Happy
Landing!

Capt Ron Nielsen

HOW TO OVERCOME FEAR OF FLYING

*A Practical Guide to Change the Way
You Think about Airplanes,
Fear and Flying:*

*Learn to Manage Takeoff, Turbulence,
Flying over Water, Anxiety
and Panic Attacks*

Capt Ron Nielsen

Editor-in-Chief: Sue Wiley
Copy Editor: Diane Owens
Layout Editor: Dieter Staudinger / Global Wellness Media
Illustrator: Theresia Staudinger
Cover Design: Eric D. Groleau / Global Wellness Media

ISBN:
Paperback: 978-1-7333385-0-9
PDF: 978-1-7333385-1-6
ePub: 978-1-7333385-2-3
Audiobook: 978-1-7333385-3-0
Kindle: 978-1-7333385-4-7

Publisher:
Global Wellness Media
Toronto • Montreal • Los Angeles
www.GlobalWellnessMedia.com

DEDICATION

To my seventh-grade teacher, James Sennett, who taught me that if we thought big enough thoughts, there was a whole world outside Jackson Township, the small rural Indiana community where I grew up. That formed the foundation for my fearless pursuit of knowledge and wisdom.

And to all the fearful flyers who have yet to realize that there is a world beyond their fears.

DISCLAIMER

None of the information contained in this book—whether it is my own opinion, the opinion of the experts in this book or the additional resources made available—constitutes or substitutes for psychological, psychotherapeutic or medical advice.

I disclaim all responsibility, loss, or risk, personal or otherwise, that is incurred as a consequence, directly or indirectly, of the use and application of any of the contents of this book or any additional resources that have been made available.

ENDORSEMENTS

What Former Fearful Flyers Say About Capt Ron

"Thank you! Thank you! I was a fearful flyer and my niece was getting married in Hawaii in October. I began my search for something, anything that could help me get on that plane and not lose my mind. I found your fearless flight class. We took the flight to Las Vegas after the first seminar and I did very poorly on the first flight. I was disappointed, discouraged and thought I can never do this. Captain Ron assured me I would do better on the flight back to Phoenix. I did it and I felt triumphant! Still worried about an 8-hr. flight. My husband got the Harmonizer for me and I used it faithfully before the flight. The day of our flight it was a lifesaver! My husband and I couldn't believe the difference in my ability to fly and not be terrified. There was once during heavy turbulence that I got a little nervous, but I put on my Harmonizer and got through it. Captain Ron, you are a lifesaver!!! We're planning our next trip. Words cannot convey my gratitude!"

—SYLVIA C.

✳ ✳ ✳

"Thank you for what you do to help those that are afraid of flying. Your program and techniques work. I have witnessed it first-hand watching my wife Mary transform in a most remarkable way. She gained confidence and the knowledge she needed to get on the plane. Your generosity with your time and genuine positive coaching is very refreshing. What you do really makes a difference.

Mary really trusted you and used the Harmonizer and it worked. She would tune in each week on Facebook and found a place where she felt comfortable and common issues with others that she could relate to. Fearless Flight is the way to go when you need help in overcoming the fear of flying. Thanks Captain Ron!"

—DANE G.

＊ ＊ ＊

"Captain Ron you are the best! I didn't fly for over 20 years due to fear of flying...but now I have flown to New York last summer and to Oregon in the Fall and now to four of the Hawaiian Islands in July...

I am still nervous, but it doesn't take control of me anymore...I have learned to take control of my fear and it is greatly due to your Cleared for Takeoff class. I really, really felt that life and adventure would pass me by if I didn't get "onboard". Literally, ha! But seriously, your Cleared for Takeoff class two years ago was my ticket to live life to the fullest again.

The part of just sitting on the static plane with others and talking and laughing was incredibly valuable to me. When I got on planes while traveling, I remembered how comfortable I felt in the class and held on to that feeling! I found my confidence again - and now I know I can do it! Thank you so much for giving me part of my life back. I am forever grateful! Keep doing what you are doing! You are making a huge difference in people's lives! Keep up the great work!"

—KAREN M.

＊ ＊ ＊

FOREWORD

Throughout the global aviation industry, the safety and security of customers, team members and aircraft are always the top priority. While airlines around the world compete on products and routes, we don't compete on safety.

Despite all the changes that have occurred in the airline industry in recent years, one thing that has remained constant is an unwavering commitment to safety. Airlines have a vested interest in running a safe operation because nothing ranks higher than safety in the eyes of travelers choosing an airline. Safety is at the forefront of every decision airlines make, and our team members are safety professionals first and foremost. The airline industry continues to evolve, but it never compromises safety.

Even with this steadfast focus on safety and security and the industry's excellent safety record, some people are hesitant to fly. The idea of traveling by air—a big metal tube flying 35,000 feet off the ground at 500 miles per hour—seems daunting to them. For those people who can't bear the thought of getting on an airplane, it's my pleasure to introduce you to Capt Ron Nielsen. Capt Ron is not only a veteran pilot with more than 20,000 hours of flight time, but an expert in the area of psychology and fear of flying.

I first got to know Capt Ron during our time together at America West Airlines, where he led the airline's human factors program for flight crews. The program integrated organizational development and social psychology to improve the safety of flight operations. During that time, he also began working with people who had a fear of flying.

Using his proven FearlessFlight® method, Capt Ron has helped thousands of flyers overcome their fear of air travel. He has a deep understanding of flying anxiety—what it is, what it's like to grapple with it, and how to get over it through a simple and pragmatic approach.

This book offers a practical guide to help those with a fear of flying.

The world is an amazing place, and air travel makes it much smaller and more accessible. Air travel also remains the absolute safest mode of transportation in the world.

It's my sincere hope that this book will help anyone who experiences anxiety with air travel so they will be free to fly whenever and wherever they choose.

DOUG PARKER
Chairman and CEO
American Airlines

THIS IS YOUR CAPTAIN SPEAKING

I was several years into my aviation career before I discovered that there were millions of people in the USA alone who were afraid to fly. Estimates vary widely, between 2.5 percent and 40 percent of the population—lower numbers using professionally diagnosed statistics and higher numbers when self-reported.

On an August evening in 1987, I spent two hours at a fear of flying class, volunteering to answer questions the class wanted to ask a pilot.

I thought maybe some of the people at the class might be a little nervous when flying. I had no idea until their questions revealed the depth of their fear. They fell into two groups: the "white-knuckle" flyers, those who flew only when they couldn't avoid it, and the "avoiders," the ones who would do anything to not have to fly.

I was deeply touched by the sincerity and vulnerability of those present. I was hooked. I've been working to help people overcome their fear of flying ever since, and it's been the most rewarding thing I've ever done.

At FearlessFlight®, my team and I have made it our mission to gather real insights and data from real fearful flyers just like yourself, so that we can become the voice for those who are anxious or afraid to fly. Together, we can bring about change.

There is a famous quote from 5-times Nobel Peace Prize nominee, Mahatma Ghandi:

> *"Be the change you wish to see in the world."*
> —MAHATMA GHANDI

So, if you are a fearful flyer, here is your opportunity to live this famous quote and contribute to real change in a matter that's meaningful to you and millions of other fearful flyers!

As I mentioned earlier, the biggest problem, when we talk about fear of flying is how to address and treat it most effectively. Current literature speaks only to general anxiety and fears related to flying. It is not able to address the specific issues and challenges of the many millions of real fearful flyers around the world.

Through your participation, this survey will help fill the gap of what the specific issues are that trigger fear of flying and what tools and strategies fearful flyers are currently using to cope.

It's our nature to feel that emotional issues are unique to us. Because of this we tend to feel isolated and alone. One of the most fundamental ways our autonomic nervous system regulates our emotional "thermostat" is through social connection and engagement.

Our experience over the past 32 years has demonstrated this without a doubt. For this reason, social collaboration is one of the three pillars of the FearlessFlight® Method.

The most commonly uttered remark when people participate in our Cleared for Takeoff Classes is, "What a relief to find out that I am not the only one!"

"I thought I was the only one!"

So why should you take your time to participate?

Contributing your data will:

1. Increase the development of new, more effective treatment approaches and services for fearful flyers
2. Provide critical and current data for mental health providers
3. Help create more understanding for airlines about fear of flying and how to best serve the needs of fearful flyers

Help find answers to the same questions you might have:

- How does your fear of flying compare with that of others?
- Have your fear-of-flying symptoms increased or decreased over time?
- How severe is your fear compared to that of others?
- What are the main thoughts that keep going through your head?
- What are other fearful flyers currently doing to cope?
- What external events and circumstances contribute to your fear of flying?
- How exactly is fear of flying affecting people's relationships, and personal and professional lives?

So, please take the few moments it will take to complete this survey and be part of the change that you wish to see!

Fear of Flying Research Study

Join thousands of fearful flyers and complete this Survey!

- Help find important answers about fear of flying
- Contribute to faster and more effective treatment options
- Increase awareness and service by airlines for fearful flyers

http://flf.link/BKBONUS-SURVEY

Lastly, I have observed that books on overcoming fear of flying can be too long, too boring, too vague or simply not relevant or practical. Most of them talk about flying, air traffic control and maintenance, and the psychology of fear of flying—the easy and fun stuff to talk about.

But they don't really provide guidance about what you can do to recognize, regulate and eventually replace your anxiety triggered by flying or just the thought of flying, with the freedom of directing your attention to where you choose.

Overcoming your fear requires commitment and perseverance. It helps if you love learning. It really helps if you're curious and love learning about yourself.

My goal in writing this book is to help you overcome your fear of flying.

Happy Landings!

Capt Ron

HOW TO READ THIS BOOK

You are probably reading this book because you don't feel safe flying on an airplane. You are likely someone who hasn't ever flown, avoids flying at all costs, or is a "white-knuckle" flyer. But don't beat yourself up about it. There is a reason for this fear, and it starts in the brain.

The purpose of this book and why I wrote it, is to help you change the way you think which causes you to be afraid to fly.

We do this by:

1. Making you aware of how your thoughts work to hopefully give you insights that they are NOT your thoughts and you can change the way you think.

2. Making you aware of the way you currently think about flying to hopefully change myths that you have about airplanes and aviation.

3. Provide concrete tools and strategies that you can use to intervene in your current thinking to change the way that you think and manage your fear.

Through systematic discussions throughout this book, I hope to move you through the FearlessFlight® Method of education, disruption of negative thoughts, and using social engagement (the primary way that our autonomic nervous system clams us during times of arousal) to help you learn to feel safe.

FREE BOOK UPDATES AND ONLINE VIDEO CLASSES

✔ This book is INTERACTIVE - throughout the book and at the end of chapters you will have the opportunity to dive deeper into the areas that interest you most.

✔ We also update this book frequently. If you want to be notified when we release book updates as well as get free resources emailed to you please scan the QR Code or visit:

http://flf.link/BKBONUS-UPDATES

OK, let's get started.

 If you haven't completed the research survey yet, please take a moment to head over to http://flf.link/HTOFOF-SURVEY **and take inventory where you are at right now when it comes to your Fear of Flying. Alternatively, you can scan the QR code below with your smartphone or tablet.**

The questions in the survey are designed to, through your participation, evoke the parts in your brain that will allow you to absorb the content in the book on a much deeper and effective level.

CONTENTS

PART 1
THE PSYCHOLOGY OF FEAR OF FLYING

PART 2
THE BASICS OF FLIGHT

PART 3
COPING TOOLS AND STRATEGIES

PART 1

THE PSYCHOLOGY OF
FEAR OF FLYING

Part 1 of the book is written to help make you aware of how your thoughts work to hopefully give you insights that your thoughts are NOT your thoughts and you can change the way you think.

When You Are Finished with Part 1, You Will:

1. Understand fear of flying is an anxiety disorder – a dis-ease – and not a character flaw. You are not crazy, and you can overcome your fear!

2. Analyze the way you think in order to **recognize, regulate and replace** your mental dialogue with the facts and information you need to fly fearlessly.

3. Evaluate your triggers to create healthy responses to things that go "bump" in your flight.

CHAPTER 1

HOW YOU GOT HERE

"If you are what you eat, what does that say
about what goes through your mind?"

—CAPT RON

Born to Worry

Thinking, what is it good for? I like to say that question to the tune of the Edwin Starr's recording of "War." If you're not familiar with the pounding beat to that song popular during the Vietnam War era, my mention not only won't resonate with you, but it may even cause you to wonder why the heck I put this somewhat illogical reference right here in the opening to my book.

But that's the point, thoughts come and go through our minds all the time. Often without any apparent connection to those thoughts that preceded them—and very often causing others to question our logic. Logic and rationality happen to be contextual.

It is in fact our ability to think which defines our specialness as a species. I'm talking about the process of what we notice in our conscious awareness as we motor through the day. In my mind, this is different from just being conscious.

There's a lot of debate about what constitutes consciousness. I don't want to get sucked into that debate, so I'm attempting to get your agreement that we can use the word "consciousness" to describe the state of having thoughts and the word "mindfulness" as the awareness of the state of being aware that we're having thoughts—rather like being one's own observer. And crazy as it sounds, the mind has a mind of its own.

And, boy, do we have thoughts! I don't know how anyone would have been able to figure this out, but I've read that the average human being has between 50,000 and 60,000 thoughts a day. Using the low number of 50,000 and considering how many seconds there are in a day, this comes down to having one thought every 1.72 seconds. If you allow eight hours for sleeping (don't even get me started on dreaming), now you're down to 1.15 seconds for each thought.

You might have already thought (pun attempted), "I never thought about that!" So, back to my original question, "Thinking, what is it good for?" Think about it. (Gotcha' again!) And you better hurry because you've got to squeeze in another 49,998 more thoughts to meet your minimum daily quota.

By now perhaps you're thinking, "This is what I paid for?"

Hang in there with me. There's a lot more wisdom where this came from. There's a lot more wisdom that I've accumulated from others, much more thoughtful (it just keeps getting better, doesn't it!) than I am on the subject.

We didn't originally come with equipment to do the kind of thinking that sets us apart from other "lower" animals. One benchmark puts this modification to our brain as having taken place between 200 million to 360 million years ago. It doesn't really matter that much for our purposes here except to establish that the way we think began to change into more the way we do it today.

Imagine our ancestors walking across the savannas of Africa a couple million years ago. Let's call one of them Rudy and the other Eugene. They hear a rustling in the tall grass. Rudy says, *"Aw, it's probably just the wind,"* and keeps on walking.

Eugene, on the other hand, isn't buying it. He's skeptical. He cuts a wider berth. Before you know it, a lion jumps out and eats Rudy. Rudy gets taken out of the gene pool. And Eugene is able to escape by running away. Eugene has what I call the worry gene. And that's what you and I inherited, Eugene's worry gene. And it's kept us alive for millions of years.

Although the threats that Rudy and Eugene faced are no longer as widespread or potentially as lethal, our worry gene remains just as alert as it was for these prehistoric ancestors. And the brain's response to those threats, whether real or imagined, remains much the same as it did for Rudy and Eugene.

We Worry About Everything

Why do we worry? Because it's our nature—our nature to survive. That's the Number One responsibility of our brain—to keep us alive. Worry is all biological. You don't have a say in when you get triggered. It's all automatic. We're going to go into that in a little more detail in Chapter 2, but for now, I want to talk more about our thinking in general, and why we are convinced that our thinking is logical and rational but seems so contradictory not only some of the time, but much of the time.

At this point, your logical thought may be: so, what does all this have to do with fear of flying?

Why Fear of Flying Defies Logic

If you believe that flying is inherently dangerous, then it will always be a filter through which you judge all things flying. Let's say you're reading through a newspaper or more likely, your newsfeed. You come across a headline that says,

"Airplane Strikes Jet Bridge Causing Damage to Wingtip." You have an immediate and visceral reaction; the intensity of this reaction depends only on how triggered you get.

That ever-present little voice in your head says, *"See, I told you. Flying is for the birds!"* Forget about the fact that if you go deeper into the article you would see that the damage occurred as a result of a mechanic repositioning the airplane to a new gate and not properly clearing the pathway.

Nor are you likely to do a deep dive to discover that each day there are some 105,000 commercial flights that take off and land without incident. Why is that?

* * *

BELIEFS AND BEHAVIORS AS HABITS

Our preference for the hand with which we write isn't the only thing we do out of habit. We have preferences for the way we think and behave. The way we think is a habit.

If I were to ask you, *"How much is 2 plus 2?"* You would answer 4 without hesitation. If I asked you, *"What is 24 time 17?"* you would likely not be able to answer without some delay—not because you aren't good at math per se, but because computing the answer to this second problem requires you to use a different thinking process.

At any given time, our behavior is the interplay between two modes or systems of thinking. As Daniel Kahneman, the 2002 Nobel Prize winner for his work in creating the field of behavioral economics (really social psychology), describes in Thinking Fast and Slow, our beliefs and our behaviors often contradict each other.

The so-called System 1 thinking is fast, intuitive, effortless, and completely unreflected. Things we learn to do automatically feel like we do them without thinking.

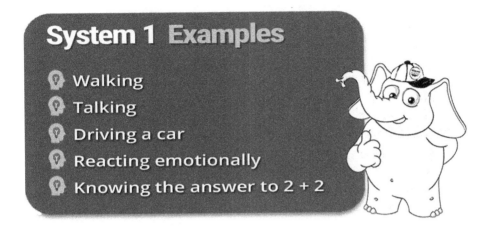

System 2 is the brain's slower, more deliberate, effortful, and analytical mode. System 2 doesn't do two plus two, but it picks up responsibility for 17 times 24. It gets involved in difficult life decisions, in self-control, and sometimes, in checking and correcting intuition.

The main thing about System 1, Kahneman says, is that it can't be turned off.

The main thing about System 2, even though we might imagine it to be the "real," conscious us, is that it's lazy. It's very capable of endorsing and rationalizing what our fast thinking is telling us to do and say. Effort and attention are very closely related to consciousness (conscious awareness is the term I choose to use).

When you multiply 17x24, you are operating in sequence and are aware of the sequence, so you are aware that you are thinking.

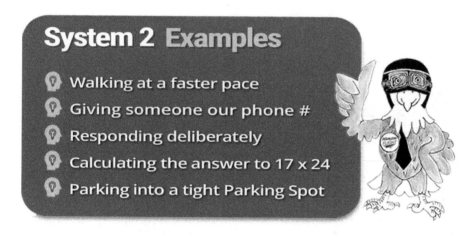

System 2 Examples

- Walking at a faster pace
- Giving someone our phone #
- Responding deliberately
- Calculating the answer to 17 x 24
- Parking into a tight Parking Spot

With System 1, however, you are NOT aware that you are thinking.

This is a definition of intuition; you know something without knowing why you know it.

Another name for intuition is procedural learning.

Using procedural learning specific behaviors become skilled and second nature.

What used to be effortful and a function of System 2, now becomes automatic and a function of System 1.

What used to be slow becomes fast.

Why You Can't Believe Everything You Believe

Our beliefs do not come from where we think they come. When asked what you believe, whether you believe in climate change or not or some political position, as soon as the question is raised you have answers. Reasons come to your mind, but they have very little to do with the real causes of your beliefs.

The real reasons for your beliefs are rooted in your personal history — in the people that you trusted and what they seemed to believe in.

It has very little to do with the reasons that come to mind in any current moment. And furthermore, we take those reasons much too seriously.

* * *

SYSTEM 1 VS SYSTEM 2

The Elephant vs the Rider – The Original Odd Couple

A metaphor that I first read in Jonathan Haidt's book, *The Righteous Mind*[1] uses an Elephant and a Rider as a metaphor to describe the separate functions for System 1 and System 2. Imagine a rider on an elephant whose role is to serve the elephant.

The rider represents our conscious reasoning — the effortful part of our thinking of which we are totally aware. Haidt maintains that the elephant represents the other 95 percent of our thinking — the part that actually controls our behavior, but which we may not be aware of.

Together they represent an odd couple who work together — not always in harmony — but together as we try to navigate life in search of meaning and connection.

---

[1] Jonathan Haidt, *The Righteous Mind: Why Good People Are Divided by Politics and Religion.* (Knopf Doubleday Publishing Group. Kindle Edition.)

SYSTEM 1   SYSTEM 2

Characteristics

SYSTEM 1	SYSTEM 2
Intuition & Instinct	Rational Thinking
Slow Thinking	Fast Thinking
Unconscious	Conscious
Automatic	Effortful
Impulsive	Reflective
Associative	Logical
95%	5%

Source: Daniel Kahneman

The Rider's (System 2) attempt to use deliberate thinking requires effort. On the other hand, the Elephant (System 1), which dominates our thought processes and is sometimes cumbersome, seemingly moves effortlessly.

Ironically when we get our Elephant to slow down our thinking, we become much more aware of it since this draws our attention to the fact that we are being effortful. It leads us to believe that our Rider is much more in control than he is.

Consequently, it stifles our search for the deep truth about issues. The immediate consequence for someone who has a fear of flying is that they end up believing in myths about flying that perpetuate and aggravate their fears.

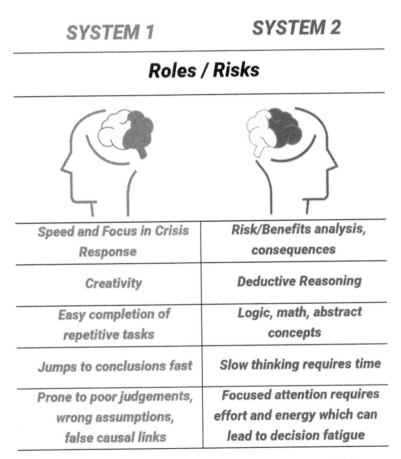

SYSTEM 1	SYSTEM 2
Roles / Risks	
Speed and Focus in Crisis Response	Risk/Benefits analysis, consequences
Creativity	Deductive Reasoning
Easy completion of repetitive tasks	Logic, math, abstract concepts
Jumps to conclusions fast	Slow thinking requires time
Prone to poor judgements, wrong assumptions, false causal links	Focused attention requires effort and energy which can lead to decision fatigue

Source: Daniel Kahneman

Effort and attention are very closely related to consciousness. Because Rider thinking (System 2) requires more effort, and again, we notice it more, and this causes us to believe our Rider is in control and we're using our more logical and rational mind.

So, when you multiply 24 by 17, you become aware of being deliberate and operating in sequence and you are therefore much more aware of your thinking than you are when using your Elephant brain, which is intuitive in nature.

Your Elephant brain is not aware of the thinking. What it's doing is what defines intuition—knowing without knowing why you know it. But, when we practice using the more effortful Rider brain, we become skilled, not unlike learning to add two plus two.

And before you know it, what used to be effortful and directed by our Rider becomes automatic and part of our Elephant brain. What used to be "slow thinking" now becomes fast.

* * *

THE STORIES WE TELL OURSELVES

E + R = O

Perhaps the most problematic facet of System 1 is that it generates stories to justify its beliefs. It looks for causes that, if endorsed by our Rider, become beliefs and opinions. This is a huge pitfall for the truth sometimes—like if you have a fear of flying. The speed at which we find explanations for things that happen can make it difficult for us to learn the deep truth—such as what the true nature is of all those unfamiliar sights, sounds, and sensations as opposed to whatever our Elephant makes up as a story. And making up stories is what we do.

Here's a formula I teach my students to explain how stories can influence and even dominate our state of mind.

From time to time in my Cleared for Takeoff Classes, I'll select someone to demonstrate how the formula in Figure 1 works.

> **E** is an event in life.
>
> **R** is your response to that event, or what is really
>
> the story that you tell yourself about the event.
>
> **O** is the outcome.

I'll begin my demonstration by explaining the formula. For any given Event that happens to us in life, we add our response or a story about that event, which then determines the outcome. Since we can't control the things that happen to us in life, the only thing we can control is our response, which is often a story that we generate. I've represented the letter *R* larger than the E and the O because that's symbolic of the R's importance.

Then I look directly at the subject and say, "*You know, Jim. I've been helping people overcome their fear of flying since 1987. During that time, I've seen thousands of people go through my classes. I have to be honest; I think that you're not likely to be successful as you don't seem to have what it takes."*

People often laugh nervously at first because they are somewhat shocked by the frankness and negative tone of my narrative. I then turn to the class and ask, *"Now using this formula, after listening to my critique, will Jim's self-esteem go up or down?"*

I ask for a show of hands and inevitably a majority think that Jim's self-esteem will go down. I then point out that the correct answer is, "It depends on the story that Jim tells himself following my criticism." I go on to explain that if Jim takes what I said literally to heart, his self-esteem may very well go down. But if Jim reasons that I picked him because I thought he was a good sport and we had developed a little rapport already in class, his self-esteem will probably go up.

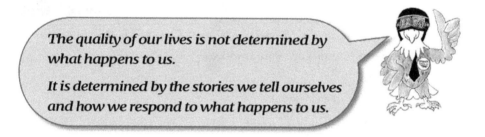

The quality of our lives is not determined by what happens to us.

It is determined by the stories we tell ourselves and how we respond to what happens to us.

Most fearful flyers blame the airplane, or the turbulence, or closing the door, or the length of the flight, or any number of external factors for their anxiety about flying. We have seen how our beliefs are supported by our thinking and specifically the stories that we tell ourselves to justify those beliefs.

We must recognize the stories that we've been telling ourselves to go beyond our limiting beliefs.

* * *

THE BRAIN CREATES STORIES

Your Brain creates stories from your beliefs which you create about why it's unsafe to fly. Experiencing the effects of these beliefs not only creates your attitude which influences your actions. This in turn perpetuates and strengthens the thoughts that fuel the beliefs of why it is justified to be afraid to fly.

Left unchecked, you can now appreciate how your fear and the emotional and physical symptoms have only become stronger over time, as you practiced this pattern.

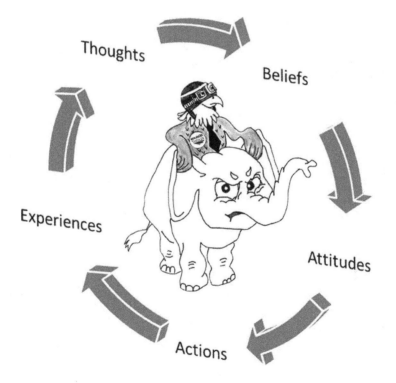

Of course, you didn't willfully or consciously "practice" your anxiety about flying but the result is all the same.

The story of one of my students comes to mind. It illustrates the process I have just laid out for you.

NO 523 | NAME NOM **Mary M, GA**
Belief Cycles

FEARLESSFLIGHT®
CASE FILES

"I used to fly all the time, like I never thought about it, but I had some type of anxiety or panic attack... I went up to the flight attendant so I could get off. She promptly told me to go back to my seat.

There was some turbulence and I felt like very claustrophobic. You realize how high up we were, and it started going through my head and then I started having trouble breathing and they told her I need to get up. I think I'm dying. I later discovered it was like a panic attack of some sort. And so, I think that kind of set off my whole year. I was visiting my dad; I was out here going to school and I told him I never wanted to fly again, and could I please take the train back? So, he got me a train ticket. Now looking back, I'm going to be 50. I had an amazing dad, but I wish he would've just said no."

This was how Mary's experience with fear of flying begins. It's full of stories from her reaction to her breathing to the response from the flight attendant. It helps to explain how she got to where she was when I first talked to her.

Her story about flying may not be so different from how you got to where you are today. But no matter what got you here, your fear of flying directly relates to your beliefs about flying and the stories you tell yourself that result in feeling unsafe.

* * *

OUR BRAIN'S #1 PRIORITY IS TO KEEP US ALIVE.

The brain uses thinking to accomplish that.

Thinking is what we do as humans. But sometimes our best thinking gets us into trouble.

We form beliefs first, and then work out the details to support those beliefs. The brain uses stories to create narratives that describe and make sense of our experiences.

Our stories determine the kind of experience we will have because they form the basis not only for our beliefs, but also our attitudes, values, goals, and motivations that form the filters of our perceptions.

In Part 3 you will find a <u>downloadable</u> **E + R = O Activity sheet**.

It is important for you to take the time and get clarity on your triggers. This is vital because we need to become mindful of the first signs in your body as well as your preceding thoughts, **<u>before</u>** your elephant has taken charge and takes you for a ride.

KEY TAKEAWAYS

- Life is not what happens to you.
- It's about the story you tell yourself that defines your experiences.
- If you want a better experience, you must have a better story!
- Change your story, change your experience.

As you continue on in the book, one story that you could be telling yourself, if you are not from the Arizona or California area, is this: *"Oh, I wish I could attend one of Capt Ron's free introductory and/or advanced classes."*

There is absolutely no doubt that these classes are powerful and if you have any means to get to one of our classes, I highly encourage you to do so. However, over the past 32+ years I have helped far more people who located anywhere but Arizona and California.

Regardless of your locale, we have recorded one of our Cleared for Takeoff 101 Classes at Phoenix Sky Harbor Airport and edited it into 9 shorter video segments for easy consumption.

You can gain free access to the Cleared for Takeoff 101 Online Video Class in our FearlessFlight® Hub, along with other free resources for you. You will find information on how to access the Class for free at the end of this chapter.

You may be wondering why I decided to give away so many free resources. The answer is simple. Overcoming your fear of flying is a process and the more tools you have in your toolkit the better you will be prepared. And what gets me out of bed at 72 years old is the lives that change whenever someone overcomes their fear of flying!

We have most likely not met yet, so it is impossible for me to know where on your journey you find yourself as you are reading this book.

For some, this book is all they need to manage and overcome their fear. For most, the journey may require a little more effort and sustained attention in implementing the tools and strategies that you will learn about in this book.

Think of choosing to learn a new language. Because it's new, it could be more difficult at the start. It gets easier the more you practice it. And the more you practice, the better you get at it. However, what happens when you learned a language and then you don't use it for a while? We tend to get rusty.

Most of us don't fly regularly enough and so staying connected to like-minded and like-hearted people who not only have empathy for our challenges but are - or have been - where we are at this point, when it comes to your fear of flying, is crucial to our success.

So, I hope that offering you access to this free Cleared for Takeoff 101 Class online gives you the opportunity to dive deeper and thereby get closer to your goal!

You can gain access to the class, as well as the other free resources we have created for you by scanning the QR Code or typing the link below into your browser on your smartphone, tablet or computer.

FREE CLASS!

Watch and enjoy a recording of one of our free LIVE classes at the Phoenix Sky Harbor Airport, right from the comfort of your living room. You'll get 9 videos in total, so you can also fit them in on the go.

http://flf.link/BKBONUS-HUB

* * *

CHAPTER 2

THE BIOLOGY OF FEAR

"You Can't Solve an Inside Problem
with an Outside Solution"

—CAPT RON

In Chapter one we learned that our mind has a mind of its own. We think that we know what we know, but that is not the case. Here in Chapter 2, you will see that there is a complete biological process that kicks into action once your survival instinct is activated.

NO 1259 | NAME NOM **Kelly L, CA**
Fear and Anxiety

FEARLESSFLIGHT®
CASE FILES

"My first flight was in eighth grade. I don't recall having a fear of flying at that time. We actually flew through a lightning storm and I thought it was the coolest thing ever. That's the difference between an eight and 25-year old. The changing point was when I was in high school, I watched a movie called The Final Destination.

In the movie, there's an explosion on the plane during takeoff. It was very real and it triggered something in me and really messed me up to the point whenever I would get on an airplane, that's all I could think of when we would be taking off.

So, any time I would get ready to fly--probably about a week before I my flight, I would sleep only about two to three hours because it was all could think about. And sometimes, I would have anxiety attacks any time I would think about my upcoming flight. During the drive to the airport, I would be shaking. I was so afraid."

Once I got to the airport, I would immediately go to the bar and get a glass of wine and just try to not think about flying. But of course, as soon as I would hear, "Okay, we're loading all passengers," I would walk down the tarmac and get on the plane, and that's just where it all really started. As soon as the door closed, I felt trapped. I felt stuck and so out of control of the situation. It was just terrifying. I would squeeze my husband's hand. I felt like crying. It would take me a good hour into the flight to just really calm down and be able to enjoy it. I would be exhausted because of all the stress I put myself through.

The [Cleared for Takeoff 201] class in Burbank helped tremendously when I met 35+ like-minded people who I had empathy with — they were just like me! And that alone just made me feel much better.

* * *

Do you ever feel like you're the only one who's afraid to fly? Or perhaps, your fear is the worst? In Kelly's case, she found out she was not alone.

Relax! All those people you see boarding or on the plane who look calm and collected…

Forget it! They're not all the way they appear. They are as skilled as you are in hiding their anxiety. That same part of the brain that you are worried will abandon you in your time of panic is the part that won't let you have a breakdown and embarrass yourself.

I've had many, many fearful flyers share that their biggest fear is not being able to handle their emotions. None of them have ever actually experienced that, however.

From my experience, when I meet a group of three people and they hear what I do, one of them will be afraid to fly, and another will know someone who is!

What you don't realize is that if you could see yourself during those times you feel crazy on the inside, you look just as calm to others as they look to you.

* * *

FEAR VS ANXIETY

Fear

Imagine you're on a camping trip. You open your tent flap, there's a bear staring right at you. That's Fear. Real and present danger and you have to figure out a plan of action to give you the best chance to survive.

Anxiety

You manage to successfully evade the bear and make it home safely. For the next month, you have trouble sleeping and keep replaying the camping scenario over and over thinking all the "what ifs" in the world about what might have happened had things not worked out like they did. That's anxiety!

The problem is that the part of the brain that triggers our survival instinct doesn't recognize the difference between REAL threats and imagined threats. And it uses the same biological process to react.

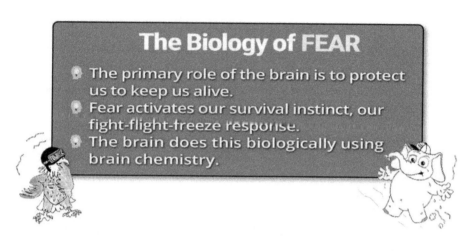

The Biology of FEAR
- The primary role of the brain is to protect us to keep us alive.
- Fear activates our survival instinct, our fight-flight-freeze response.
- The brain does this biologically using brain chemistry.

* * *

PATHWAYS TO ANXIETY

Anxiety starts either in the Amygdala (via fight-or-flight physical sensations) or in the cortex (via thoughts). Sensory signals of an external stimulus (e.g., seeing a snake or rope, hearing a loud sound, speaking in front of a crowd) go to the thalamus, which translates and sends out two messages. In short, there are two pathways to anxiety.

The Prefrontal Cortex

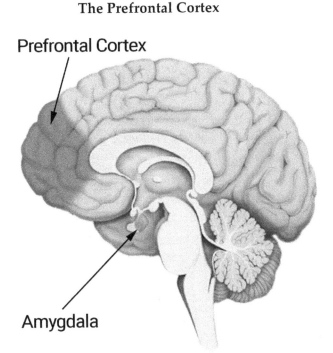

The prefrontal cortex (PFC) is located in the very front of the brain, just behind the forehead.

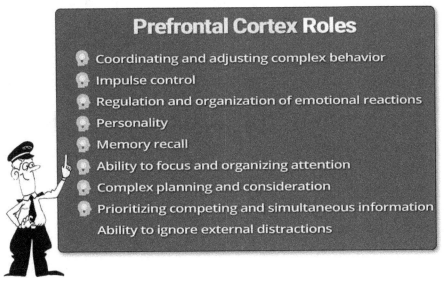

When you find yourself ruminating over the weather, turbulence or the door closing, you are likely experiencing cortex-based anxiety.

The Amygdala

The amygdala is an almond-shaped structure in the brain. The word Amygdala is the Greek word for "almond." And while the name suggests only one, we actually have two amygdalae. Each amygdala is located in the frontal portion of the temporal lobe.

The specific role of the amygdala, however, remains somewhat controversial, however, it is essential to your ability to feel certain emotions and to perceive them in other people. This includes fear and the many changes that it causes in the body. For our purposes here, when you think of the amygdala, think fear.

The amygdala is the reason we are afraid of things outside our control. It also controls the way we react to certain events, or triggers, that cause emotional reactions which we perceive as potentially threatening or dangerous.

This part of the brain creates powerful physical sensations in the body. It has numerous connections to other parts of the brain and therefore can trigger reactions very quickly. Doesn't produce thoughts that you're aware of therefore, many of the responses remain outside your conscious control.

When you find yourself saying things like, *"I know that my fear isn't logical"* or "I don't know where my fear of flying came from" you're likely experiencing anxiety initiated by the amygdala pathway.

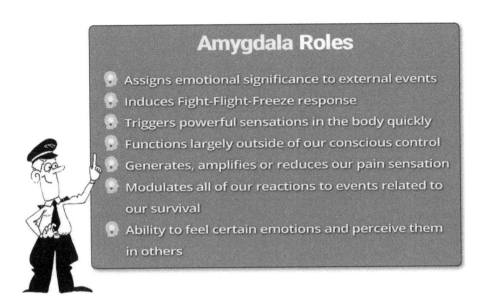

Amygdala triggers are often treated using anti-anxiety medications, which is very effective in many cases to reduce the anxiety but unfortunately does nothing to change the neuron circuitry.

The amygdala is the lookout for danger and sets off the fear alarm we know as our fight or flight response anxiety.

* * *

Here are two examples of questions a fearful flyer might ask that can trigger fight or flight behavior:

1. **What if I have a panic attack?**

2. **What if the pilots lose control?**

YOUR BRAIN WILL AUTOMATICALLY TRIGGER
YOUR FLIGHT OR FLIGHT

Have you ever noticed that "little voice" that talks to you? You might be sitting there reading this right now and thinking, "*Do I talk to myself? I don't think I talk to myself.*" That's the little voice I'm talking about. It's always present, especially in times of self-doubt or anxious moments.

Who's Doing the Talking?

The constantly talking voice inside people's heads is not actually them. It is just a voice that they hear in their minds and recognize through their consciousness.

A person's inner voice employs a selective process while interpreting the world around them to create their own version of reality in their minds. This mental model of reality can act as a buffer for the person to protect against the parts of the world around them that they do not like or agree with. This mental model, however, is not actual reality itself.

On the following page is an illustration of two examples about what can happen with the amygdala (fear center) and the cortex when you see a danger that isn't real.

The fearful flyer sometimes gets stuck.

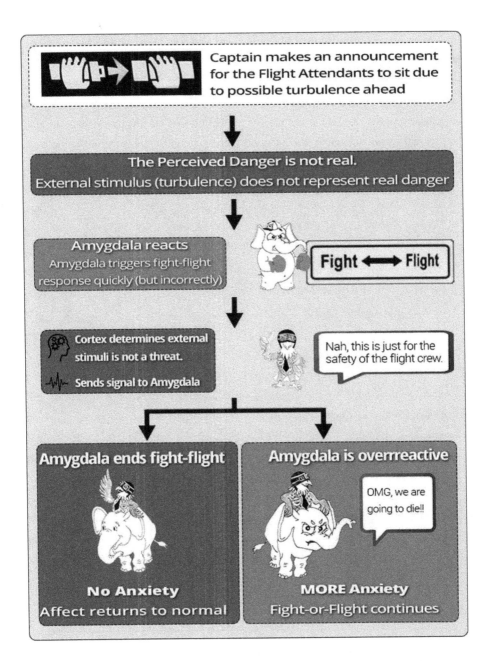

The challenge for the fearful flyer is breaking the chain of events in the brain which lead to more and anxiety and discomfort. It can be done sometimes by distraction or influx of correct information that ultimately replaces these reoccurring thoughts and patterns. We will discuss this further in Part 3.

We've established that no matter whether the threat is real or imagined, once the Amygdala is triggered a biological process is initiated that sets in motion all a range of physical and emotional responses that are difficult if not impossible to contain without removing the threat or removing one's self from the threat.

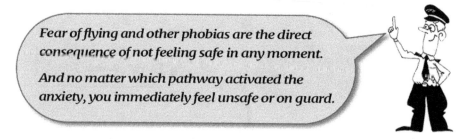

Fear of flying and other phobias are the direct consequence of not feeling safe in any moment.

And no matter which pathway activated the anxiety, you immediately feel unsafe or on guard.

Remember that worry gene we talked about in Chapter 1?

When we were born, that worry gene was alive and well. Most of us entered the world immediately in an elevated arousal state evidenced by exercising our lungs as we cried. That is an inherent ability within all of us. We knew how to get upset as a means to communicate to caregivers that something was wrong, and we needed help.

Upset means that we knew how to elevate our bodily functions, our blood pressure or heart rate and all those things to get us ready to either fight or flee. What we didn't come with the automatic ability to do was to calm ourselves down—to reverse this arousal. That had to come from our caregivers. In most cases, it's Mom who first teaches us how to self-soothe and calm ourselves down.

There are three primary signals that we received:
Touch, Tone of Voice, and Gaze.

The very first act for a newborn is usually to be held and caressed. Often gentle touch is accompanied by sounds of mom's voice saying, *"there, there...it's okay."* And all the while this intimate dialogue is continuing, Mom is gazing into our eyes lovingly smiling. These are our first experiences with social engagement.

Social engagement is one of the most powerful forces among human beings. If we were cared for in these ways, we enjoyed a healthy attachment and began to learn how to calm ourselves down following an increase in arousal.

If our caregivers early in our life didn't get it right, we risked not learning how to calm ourselves down. The result is like a faulty thermostat in your house. It's designed to regulate the temperature within a certain range. When it gets too hot, it activates the air conditioner to bring the temperature down. If it gets too cold, it activates the heater to warm things back up.

If, however, you have a broken thermostat, when you get triggered and become anxious you have difficulty down regulating your inner state to calm yourself down. That's the nature of fear of flying—an unsolicited increase in your level of arousal from which you are unable to calm yourself.

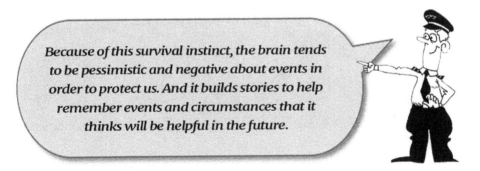

Because of this survival instinct, the brain tends to be pessimistic and negative about events in order to protect us. And it builds stories to help remember events and circumstances that it thinks will be helpful in the future.

Because of this survival instinct, the brain tends to be pessimistic and negative about events in order to protect us. And it builds stories to help remember events and circumstances that it thinks will be helpful in the future.

How else could it be that two people, both watching the same movie, can have completely different experiences? In the same way that two people getting on the same airplane can have completely different experiences.

You can't control what happens to you, but you can control the decision (the story) you make about what happens to you.

* * *

In Chapter 3, we're going to look at the two types of triggers that activate a fearful flyer's level of arousal.

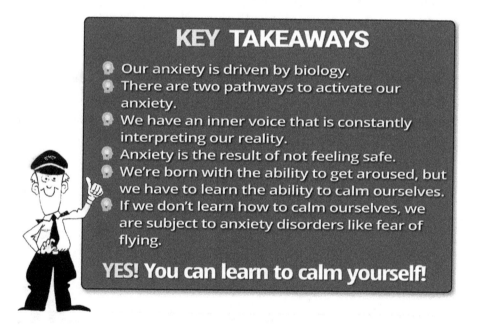

KEY TAKEAWAYS

- Our anxiety is driven by biology.
- There are two pathways to activate our anxiety.
- We have an inner voice that is constantly interpreting our reality.
- Anxiety is the result of not feeling safe.
- We're born with the ability to get aroused, but we have to learn the ability to calm ourselves.
- If we don't learn how to calm ourselves, we are subject to anxiety disorders like fear of flying.

YES! You can learn to calm yourself!

We live in a truly amazing age. The use of technology aids our ability to learn and communicate with each other around the world at the click of a button. Certainly, commercial aviation has benefitted and indeed is an innovator of technology designed to make flying safer, more efficient and more comfortable for its customers.

Given the nature of fear of flying, it is likely you may not have the option to come to one of my live Advanced Classes in Phoenix or Los Angeles. Add to that work, school, social obligations, and familial responsibilities, our lives run the risk of becoming over-scheduled at any point to easily create time to attend a class when you may not be yet convinced that you can truly fly free from fear and anxiety. Take a deep breath. You are not alone!

Thanks to this modern technology, online learning is an educational medium that allows you to participate in this MasterClass, streaming it online via the internet. This way you can choose to learn whatever applies most to you, from the comfort of your own home and on your schedule.

The MasterClass is a perfect companion to this book and will deepen your knowledge and insights you learn in these pages. You will virtually participate in the MasterClass and can ask questions right in the members' area.

Learn more and join our **Online *"How to Overcome Fear of Flying"* Video MasterClass**. Simply scan the QR Code or type the link below into your browser on your smartphone, tablet or computer.

CHAPTER 3

TRIGGERS

WHAT TRIPS YOUR TRIGGERS?

"The pain in your brain is not about the plane."

—CAPT RON

So, what bothers you about flying? What are the sights, sounds, situations, or circumstances that activate your fear center and trigger your anxiety? Triggers are external events or circumstances that produce very uncomfortable emotional or physical symptoms, such as anxiety, panic, discouragement, despair, or dread. Triggers are usually accompanied by negative mental dialogue—that little voice of doom inside your mind.

Triggers are a function of your autonomic nervous system and are activated when you don't feel safe. You'll recall from Chapter 2 that there are two pathways to anxiety: the cortex and the Amygdala.

Kathy, one of my online coaching students had a fear of heights. That was one of her triggers. She thinks it started with 9/11 and things got worse and worse from there. Thinking about being up in the air at 30,000 feet scared her. It was not being closed in but the height issue. Being that far up. Kathy's story is just one example of a trigger for some fearful flyers. I will discuss claustrophobia in more detail in Chapter 5.

There are two categories of triggers when it comes to flying: mechanical and emotional. Each represents one of the pathways to anxiety that we discussed in Chapter 2.

The point of looking at triggers is an obvious place to start how to overcome your fear of flying. Knowing what "trips your trigger" can provide insight into what you need to do.

Mechanical triggers stimulate thoughts and feelings that are related to the nuts and bolts of flying.

Emotional triggers go on in your mind such as a fear of heights and fear of enclosed spaces (claustrophobia). These triggers are automatically activated by the autonomic nervous system.

TRIGGERS

MECHANICAL	EMOTIONAL
They are "thinking" Triggers. Some examples include:	They are "feeling" Triggers. Some examples include:
Amygdala	Cortex
Takeoff	Fear of heights
Turbulence	Claustrophobia
Thunderstorms and the weather	Fear of social situations
Pilot skill and capability	Fear of germs
The airworthiness of an airplane	Superstitions
Mechanical problems and maintenance issues	Negative self-talk that fuels your fear

We are hardwired with a negativity bias—it's natural; it's how the brain protects us. Neuropsychologist Rick Hanson, Ph.D., identifies that our brains are like Teflon for the good experiences that come our way and Velcro for the negative. For example, if your boss tells you three good things about your performance and one negative thing, which one are you likely to dwell on—over and over?

The next time something like this happens to you, you know that you can blame the Velcro capacity of your brain for the misery you experience from that one comment. But if you are not aware that this one comment is the trigger for your anxious misery, perhaps your future performance will suffer because you become anxious by repeating to yourself this one negative thing.

In this example, it's easy to see that the trigger for your anxiety is the one negative comment and your brain's tendency to hang on to it.

Negative mental dialogue can fuel your fear. Using the previous example about your performance review at work, let's imagine what happens after you hear the one negative thing about your performance (and forget about the good things that your boss told you). What do you say to yourself?

Let me suggest some examples:

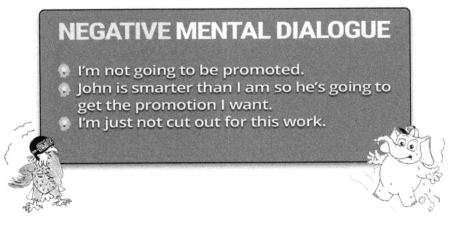

NEGATIVE MENTAL DIALOGUE

- I'm not going to be promoted.
- John is smarter than I am so he's going to get the promotion I want.
- I'm just not cut out for this work.

And it's very likely that your negative mental dialogue will evolve into a prediction of your worst-case fear: **I'm going to be fired!**

How do you think your negative mental dialogue will influence your future performance? It won't be pretty, will it? But if you can slow down your thinking and reflect on what triggers your fear of being fired, you will be able to identify the trigger as that one negative comment from your boss and the firestorm of negative mental dialogue that this comment sets off in you.

Perhaps you can then pause to remember the good things that your boss told you and reflect on those. Dr. Rick Hanson calls this practice "taking in the good." Maybe as you're stopping to savor the good things that your boss told you, you will be able to formulate a plan to increase the occurrence of these good things that your boss noticed.

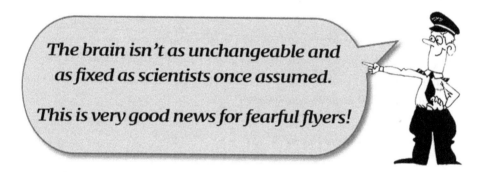

The brain isn't as unchangeable and as fixed as scientists once assumed.

This is very good news for fearful flyers!

The brain isn't fixed and unchangeable as so many people, including scientists, once assumed. The circuits of your brain aren't determined completely by genetics; they're also shaped by your experiences and the way you think and behave. This is very good news for fearful flyers!

Let's review by remembering one of my catch phrases: *"The pain in your brain is not about the plane."* So, if you can change your brain, then you can change your pain (about flying) by changing the way you think.

What is a strategy to changing the pain in your brain? As in the work performance example above, identifying the trigger of your pain is the key to choosing to do something different. Fearful flyers may not even be aware of what triggers their fear of flying, or they may be able to tell you immediately what it is that makes them anxious about flying.

Let's look at an example of the things that trigger a fearful flyer who came to my class.

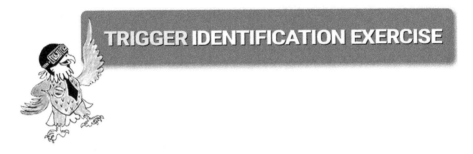

TRIGGER IDENTIFICATION EXERCISE

Sam has been flying for the last seven years, but he flies with fear and anxiety and only out of necessity for work. His coping strategy is to have a drink before he gets on the plane. As he books his flight, he can feel his pulse rate go up. When he is in the Uber, on the way to the airport, he can feel his heart in his throat. As soon as he can, he goes to the bar and has a beer. Then he heads to the boarding area.

The alcohol has calmed him down a bit. Then they announced preboarding, and Sam is still okay. Then it's his turn to board. He walks down the ramp and finds his seat. All is good. The plane taxis out and they take off. At 35,000 feet, he has another drink. Things are going smoothly until he hears a ding and sees the "fasten seatbelt sign" illuminate. He thinks, holy cow, what does that mean?

Then the pilot announces, "*Will the flight attendants please take their seats. Folks, we are going to go through some turbulence, so we've turned on the fasten your seat belt sign. Please return to your seats.*" By now Sam has begun to panic. He's anticipating that the plane will soon begin to rock all over the place. He wonders if the plane can withstand the turbulence they are about to encounter.

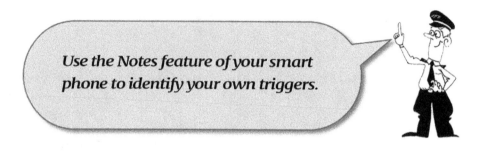

Use the Notes feature of your smart phone to identify your own triggers.

* * *

WHAT ARE YOUR TRIGGERS?

It is important to identify what scares you about flying in order for you to formulate a plan of how you will deal with your triggers. Identification of triggers is a way to begin to move out of the self-critical story of "who I am" into curiosity about "how I will respond."

Over the years, I have worked with so many fearful flyers and they've mentioned several triggers that have fueled their fear. I share some of them with you to stimulate your thinking about your own triggers. Awareness of your trigger(s) is an important key to changing your brain and therefore your response to the trigger.

Remember, a trigger is just an event that starts the whole process. It is what sets your anxiety in motion. It is the fundamental way that your autonomic nervous system responds when you feel unsafe.

Pre-flight triggers:

- Booking a flight
- Thinking about booking a flight
- Checking the weather along your flight path over and over and trying to predict what time of day will contribute to your "best" flying experience. (Stop it! ☺)
- Driving to the airport
- Going through Security
- Waiting to board
- Walking down the jetway to board the airplane
- Entering the airplane and looking down that "long metal tube"
- Changes in airflow from overhead vents
- Seeing what looks like "smoke" that seems to come from nowhere (It's really condensation when the cool cabin air meets the humid air from the local environment).
- Hearing the "barking dogs" sound (This is a sound produced by the Airbus A320 hydraulic system during pre-tax procedures. It is normal but annoying.)

In-flight Triggers:

- Waiting in line for takeoff
- Acceleration of the plane before takeoff
- The bumping sound right after the airplane leaves the ground
- First power reduction after takeoff
- Any power changes (create the illusion of climbing or descending)

- Intermediate level-offs during the climb
- The pilot changing the aircraft's direction causing it to tilt and feeling downward pressure in my seat (and sometimes you feel dizziness or disorientation
- Even the slightest amount of turbulence
- Even thinking about the possibility of turbulence
- The illumination of the fasten your seatbelt sign
- Hearing the pilot asking the flight attendants to take their seats in anticipation of upcoming turbulence (What he doesn't typically say is that this is just a precaution for their safety—not because you, the passenger, are going to die.)

Negative Mental dialogue Triggers:

- What if there are bird strikes?
- What if there's a mechanical failure?
- What if the pilot makes a mistake?
- What if the airplane isn't able to stay in the air?
- What if my flight ends up like that one crash, which I've read about— and cannot forget?
- What will happen to my children if this airplane crashes?
- What if turbulence causes this aircraft to break apart?
- What if… (fill in the worst possible consequences that your brain can imagine)?

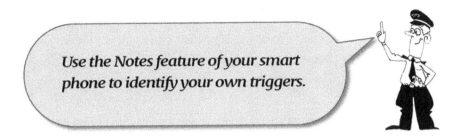

Use the Notes feature of your smart phone to identify your own triggers.

What external events or circumstances produce very uncomfortable emotional or physical symptoms for you when it comes to flying?

Take A Screen Capture of Your Triggers and Send Them to Me:

triggers@fearlessflight.com

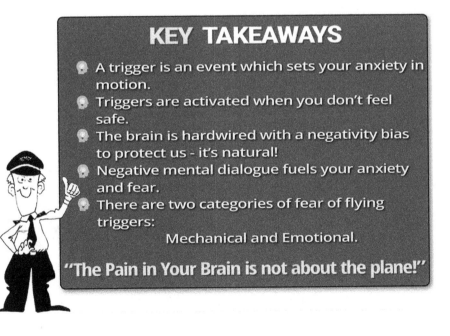

KEY TAKEAWAYS

- A trigger is an event which sets your anxiety in motion.
- Triggers are activated when you don't feel safe.
- The brain is hardwired with a negativity bias to protect us - it's natural!
- Negative mental dialogue fuels your anxiety and fear.
- There are two categories of fear of flying triggers:
  Mechanical and Emotional.

"The Pain in Your Brain is not about the plane!"

* * *

As you have learned in the first three chapters, Fear of Flying is an anxiety disorder. To overcome it you need a way to change your mental dialogue. Because you have not been able to do it by yourself, you took a step towards accomplishing your goal. You are reading this book now.

I will talk about it more in Part 3 but there is one tool that has helped thousands of fearful flyers all over the world, regulating and replacing their negative mental dialogue successfully.

The FearlessFlight® Kit. It starts the dialogue for you!

The FearlessFlight® Kit is a suite of audio, video, and document files designed as tools to be used in conjunction with the strategies of the FearlessFlight® Method which you are learning about in this book.

To let you experience the FearlessFlight® firsthand, we have created a free, complimentary 5-minute sample.

Simply scan the QR Code or type the link below into your browser on your smartphone, tablet or computer.

FREE SAMPLE

Watch and enjoy this complimentary 5-Minute FearlessFlight® Kit Harmonizer Sample.

Learn why thousands of fearful flyers swear by it.

http://flf.link/BKBONUS-FFKSAMPLE

CHAPTER 4

ANTICIPATORY ANXIETY

DON'T LET IT THROW YOU OFF — THE PLANE!

"Just because you can think it will happen
doesn't mean that it will happen."

—CAPT RON

What is Anticipatory Anxiety?

A panic attack hits suddenly, catches you by surprise, and generates your sense of threat. Our body and mind have been trained over hundreds of thousands of years to guard against harm. Toddlers don't have to burn themselves on a stove too many times before their built-in instinct trains them to watch out for stovetops.

In that same way, when you've been "burned" several times by panic, your mind searches rapidly for danger signals any time you approach a panic-provoking situation. While watching, feeling, or listening with great attention, you are on guard in case something "goes wrong" in your body or in your surroundings. Unfortunately, all this vigilance—more like hypervigilance—only contributes to your distress. You are tensing yourself up in anticipation of a problem.

Anticipatory anxiety is fear of something happening in the future.

However, the problem is, the thing you fear may never happen. In fact, when it comes to fear of flying—the crashing, dying and losing control—your worst nightmares remain a figment of your imagination and not part of your reality or your actual experience.

You worry because as I pointed out in Chapter 1, that's your nature—that's the nature of your brain—to protect you. Most problems with anxiety relate to uncertainty, and the brain does NOT like uncertainty. Your brain demands to know what to expect.

Your brain notices patterns in your environment. It then uses those patterns to predict the future and eliminate the uncertainty so that it can protect itself. It's not very good at predicting the future.

Your mind says, "*This is how it must turn out for me to feel secure. And I must feel secure.*" But there is no certainty…there are no guarantees in life. You mistakenly think in a car that you are in control. But that turns out to be an illusion as well. It is as though you require a 100 percent guarantee that you will encounter zero risk.

Isn't this a lot to ask of life? Doesn't this explain why most fearful flyers typically fear losing control?

So, ask yourself the following:

- *"Can I know for certain that I won't have any panic symptoms?"*
- *"Can I know for certain that I won't have to leave the airplane?"*
- *"Can I know for certain that I won't feel trapped?"*
- *"Can I know for certain that I won't cause an embarrassing scene on the plane?"*
- *"Can I know for certain that I won't have a panic attack on the plane?"*
- *"Can I know for certain that I won't die in a plane?"*

If you feel a strong yet inappropriate need for certainty, then confronting this problem will require that you challenge those demanding I-must-know thoughts. You will need to confront them consistently and directly every day to produce the change you want.

This is where your new attitude comes in. And your new attitude comes from changing the way you think about flying.

There's always a chance you will board an airplane and become embarrassed. There's always a chance you will have a heart attack, regardless of your health. There's always a chance you could die in a plane crash, regardless of the safety of air travel.

If you want to lower your chances of panicking and raise your chances of flying comfortably, again, we are back to changing the way you think. This book will get you started.

Basically, you have two options. You can keep telling yourself the same story. Or you can change your story. Which one will you choose?

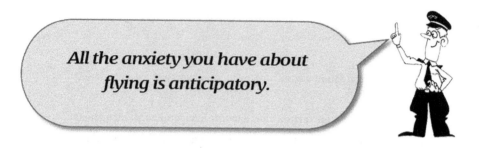

All the anxiety you have about flying is anticipatory.

We can never eliminate anticipation about the future—nor would you want to. Who wants to give up the joy in imagining your wedding day? The surprise on the face of your children on Christmas morning? Anticipating your dreams coming true? To eliminate anticipation about the future, you have to give all those up as well.

Anticipatory anxiety is the result of being able to think we can predict threats, but we can't. With great authority, it tells us things that are going to happen that are never going to happen. Yet we believe these predictions and act like they 100 percent accurate!

Since When Did You Become a Fortune Teller?

I am an old man and have known a great many troubles, but most of them never happened. Worrying is like paying a debt you don't owe. I have spent most of my life worrying about things that have never happened. Drag your thoughts away from your troubles... by the ears, by the heels, or any other way you can manage it.

—MARK TWAIN

The things we worry about <u>never</u> come to pass about 95 percent of the time and even less so when you are flying because it is so safe. How many things have you worried about that have never come to pass? What could you have done more productively instead of engaging in all this unproductive "what-if thinking?"

As Mark Twain advises, you have to "drag yourself" away from focusing on your worries and the accompanying anticipatory anxiety. When you do catch yourself engaging in what-if thinking about future events that could or may happen, bring yourself back to the present moment using your breath.

We will talk more about mindfulness in Part 3, but for now, try this simple 4/7 breath practice. Inhale to the count of 4 through your nose and exhale to the count of 7 either through your nose or mouth. Repeat several times.

The Failure to Commit

Cancelling your flight, turning around and going home instead of completing your flight, or leaving your flight before it departs all provide relief from anticipatory anxiety. And they are acceptable solutions if you never intend to fly.

The worst part is the devastation that you feel shortly after you feel the relief. And the guilt and shame build and build making it that much harder to fly the next time. The part of your brain that evolved to override the Amygdala can cause the stress hormones to stop.

But it takes courage, commitment, and perseverance. Get on the plane!

KEY TAKEAWAYS

- Anticipatory anxiety is unproductive worry about future events that are never likely to happen.
- Staying committed to overcoming your fear is the shortest path to success.

One of the best ways of dealing with anticipatory anxiety is learning more about why airplanes and flying are safe and getting your specific questions answered.

This is why we created our weekly FearlessFlight® LIVE Show. My team and I go live **every Tuesday** evening at **6:30pm Pacific** Time.

Join us and watch our Show live and, of course, watch the previous episodes as well.

They are an invaluable free resource for you. We are streaming to multiple platforms, including Facebook, YouTube and Twitter.

Simply scan the QR Code or type the link below into your browser on your smartphone, tablet or computer.

CHAPTER 5

CLAUSTROPHOBIA AND FLYING

"Most people who have a fear of flying have at least one other phobia; claustrophobia is the most common."

—CAPT RON

W hat is claustrophobia? Claustrophobia is the irrational fear of confined space. Combine that fear with the reality of being 35,000 feet in the air going 450 miles per hour, and you'll have a description of many fearful flyers' worst nightmare.

Once again, it's not the object of your thoughts that makes you afraid; it's the story you tell yourself that creates the fear. If you fear confinement and small places, boarding an airplane will be anxiety producing, no matter how composed and confident you are on land. Even a short trip can seem never ending.

For many people, fear of flying has nothing to do with worrying about the airplane crashing. Rather, flying triggers claustrophobia, which is a fear of being trapped in small, enclosed places such as an airplane cabin. Claustrophobia is really nothing more than a unique type of trigger.

While claustrophobia is sometimes mild, it can be serious enough to cause severe panic attacks, including rapid heartbeat, nausea, sweating, and lightheadedness. Taking steps to feel more in control of the situation often helps alleviate fear of flying caused by claustrophobia.

NO 768 | NAME NOM **Charles S, NY**
Claustrophobia

FEARLESSFLIGHT®
CASE FILES

Charles is a retired New York City police officer. About 10 years ago, he went on a short flight to California and just noticed things were kind of different. He began to experience claustrophobia on the plane. His heart was racing, and he couldn't wait to get off the plane. Instead of flying, he drove back home. This traumatic event stayed with him for over 10 years, and he never flew after that. At some point in his life, he was diagnosed with PTSD.

Eventually he moved to Phoenix from New York City. He had several opportunities to go back east or go on vacation. He avoided any of these opportunities because he had that thought in the back of his head, "What if I get on the plane and I have this episode? There's no escape. I'm stuck." His fear wasn't about crashing or dying. The story he told himself was that he could not have gotten get off the plane if and when he wanted to, despite confessing that this was a totally irrational fear. He basically made the decision that day 10 years ago that he wasn't going to ever get on another airplane.

Charles is someone who I think of as an avoider. In his case, he used total avoidance of his fear. If Charles' experience sounds familiar to you, you are not alone. Claustrophobia includes all that Charles experienced being in a confined place plus the fear of losing control and being embarrassed. In Charles' case, the fear started to bleed over into other parts of his life. Usually there is a pivotal event that makes you decide to get some help.

✳ ✳ ✳

HOW TO COPE WITH CLAUSTROPHOBIA

Here are some things that you can do to help you deal with claustrophobia on a plane:

Prepare in Advance

Knowing what to expect helps you feel more in control and goes a long way toward alleviating concerns about claustrophobia. Most airlines have websites that show seating diagrams. Look at the diagrams and select your seat as soon as possible.

Choose a seat where you feel most comfortable. You may prefer a seat in the front part of the plane so you can exit the plane quickly upon landing. Sitting near the front also lessens the illusion of "the long metal tube." Most people who suffer with claustrophobia prefer aisle seats, but some feel better in a window seat where they can see out. But the seat you choose depends on what works best for you.

Distract Your Mind

Take a good book, magazine, Sudoku, or crossword puzzle to occupy your mind and calm you during the flight. If you prefer not to read, take an MP3 player loaded with relaxing music or listen to an audio book. If the plane has an in-flight entertainment system, choose a light-hearted movie or comedy. Alternately, load a favorite movie on your laptop. Listen to the FearlessFlight® Harmonizer.

Breathing for Relaxation

Take a deep, slow breath through your nose, filling the bottom part of your lungs first and then the top. Concentrate on your breathing. When you breathe in, think to yourself, "I am." Finish the thought with "calm" as you exhale slowly. Imagine that your hands, shoulders, and arms are loose and relaxed. Practice deep breathing whenever you begin to feel stressed or panicky.

One technique is to breathe through a straw. You can grab one at any food court before you board. This will help to focus on your breathing, simply because you have a straw sticking out of your mouth. It also minimizes the likelihood that you will hyperventilate by breathing too rapidly and creating an imbalance of carbon dioxide. Hyperventilation is characterized by tingling and/or numbness in the fingers and toes, and lightheadedness. Some people confuse those symptoms with a lack of oxygen, which is not the case.

Avoid Stimulants

Don't drink caffeine before or during the flight. Caffeine can increase heart rate and speed your breathing, which you could misinterpret as the early signs of a panic attack. The very thought that you are starting to panic can escalate the panic further.

Eat Healthy Foods

Be sure to eat healthy foods around the time of the flight, including protein and fiber so that your blood glucose levels stay relatively stable. Sudden swings in blood glucose occur when we eat highly processed, sugary foods, and this can trigger physical symptoms like jitteriness and sweating, which can seem like the beginnings of panic.

Book the Right Seat

Which seat is best for you will depend on your unique needs. Many people with claustrophobia prefer to sit in an exit row, which provides additional leg room. Keep in mind that in order to sit here you must be reasonably physically fit and both willing and able to assist in an emergency evacuation should anything occur.

A window seat allows you to gaze outside and enjoy the view. Many people feel that this helps them to adjust their focus away from the crowded plane.

Sitting on the aisle allows you to easily move around the airplane. Walking around provides a break and can help you manage your symptoms. It also provides easier access to the restrooms, as well as to any comforting items you may have in overhead storage.

KEY TAKEAWAYS

- Unique as it is, Claustrophobia is just another trigger.
- Claustrophobia is an emotional trigger. It is ultimately caused by a story. It is not the object of your thoughts but the story you tell yourself.

Some of the best tips and tricks come from our very own FearlessFlight® Birds of a Feather family.

I created the group because I knew that social collaboration, being one of the three pillars of the FearlessFlight® Method, is really important in terms of connecting with other people, some of whom are still fearful flyers, others who have successfully overcome it and want to give back and support those still in the grip of their anxiety and fear.

Claustrophobia is a big one for many fearful flyers and so there are always active threads of people asking and answering questions. My team and I contribute every day in some form in the group but what is truly inspiring is the care, comradery and consideration that members share with and for each other.

If you would like to find out more and join, simply scan the QR Code or type the link below into your browser on your smartphone, tablet or computer.

This is a caring, safe, supportive and inclusive group that welcomes all people trying to overcome their fear of flying and want to learn more about aviation and psychology!

http://flf.link/BKBONUS-BOF

PART 2

THE BASICS OF FLIGHT

As you have learned in Part 1 of this book, there are two main types of fearful flyers.

There are those who are afraid of the technical aspects of flying, such as the safety of the plane, whether the pilots are well trained, or the mechanics and their maintenance of the airplane.

The other type of fear of flying is personal. It is internally focused and has to do with the flyer's own airworthiness and a fear within themselves, such as claustrophobia, fear of confined places, or acrophobia, the fear of heights, for example.

Regardless of what type you happen to be, I created Part 2 with the goal to arm you with just enough of the critical information and knowledge about aviation and airplanes required to allow you to generate the unshakeable confidence that airplanes and flying are safe. Part 2 will give your rider the material it requires to effectively re-regulate and replace much of the anxiety producing dialogue in you.

Once you have completed Part 2, you will know:

1. How and why airplanes fly
2. What exactly makes flying on a commercial airliner is so safe
3. How pilots, mechanics and flight attendants are trained to keep you safe
4. Everything you need to know about Turbulence and Flying over Water

CHAPTER 6

THE BASICS OF FLIGHT

HOW DOES THAT THING GET UP IN
THE AIR AND STAY THERE?

*"Give it some wings, put some engines on it, give
me a way to control it, and I'll make it fly."*

—CAPT RON

My meaningful effort to overcome your fear of flying has to include the basics of flight. You need to have some basic understanding about airplanes and flying so that you have a foundation to build your confidence that flying is safe and that you are safe.

HOW DOES A PLANE FLY?

Remember when you were a kid riding in a car and you stuck your arm out the window? Was the first thing you remember your parent saying, *"Put that arm back inside or you're going to lose it!"*

Okay, seriously, the first thing you notice is if you put the palm of your hand flat facing forward, you can feel the wind on your hand. The faster you would go, the more pressure you felt. We could actually say, the more pressure you felt on your arm, the "thicker" the air felt. If you go fast enough, the air would feel as thick as water, and if you go even faster, it would feel as thick as Jell-O.

In fact, a modern jet airplane generates heat just from the friction going over the wings. But that's not important right now. We've learned how to make the air seem "thicker" to the airplane.

✳ ✳ ✳

CONTROLLING THE FLIGHT OF A PLANE

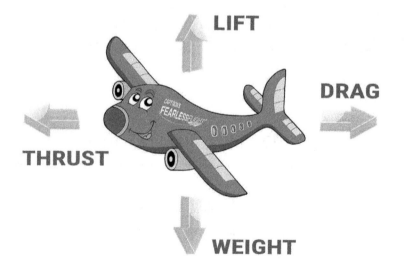

Weight is the force of gravity. It acts in a downward direction—toward the center of the Earth.

Lift is the force that acts at a right angle to the direction of motion through the air. Lift is created by differences in air pressure.

Thrust is the force that propels a flying machine in the direction of motion. Engines produce thrust.

Drag is the force that acts opposite to the direction of motion. Drag is caused by friction and differences in air pressure.

When we are flying, lift always opposes weight, and thrust is always opposite drag. All forces are in balance. For an aircraft to climb or descend, you have to increase or decrease the lift. In order for an airplane to go faster or slower, you have to increase or decrease the thrust.

Let's go back to sticking your arm out the window. Imagine putting your arm straight out with your palm facing downward parallel to the ground. Let's speed the car up to 30 mph. Now rotate the palm of your hand slightly upward and feel your arm start to "fly" up. Conversely, if you rotate the palm of your hand slightly downward, you'll feel your arm start to descend downward.

So, we know that it takes speed through the air to make the air seem thicker. And you have to angle the wing (which was represented by your hand) in order to make the wing fly.

How Does a Pilot Control the Plane?

In addition to the two main wings, we have other control surfaces that are sort of "mini-wings." One of those control surfaces is called the elevator. We manipulate it to make the airplane pitch up or pitch down. That's how we make the airplane climb or descend. When we make the nose of the airplane move up or down, we call that "pitch."

Another control surface is called the ailerons. We have one aileron on each wing. They always move opposite of each other. We turn the airplane by banking, and some of the lift that used to be going perpendicular to the ground now goes in the direction that we are banked, "pulling" the airplane in the direction that we want to turn.

To bank the airplane, the ailerons are always opposite of each other. So, when we bank to the right for a right-hand turn, the aileron on the right wing deflects up so that the right wing goes down. The aileron on the left wing deflects down so that the left wing goes up. When we make the plane bank left or right, we call that "roll."

Stick both of your arms out like you are an airplane and your arms are the wings. Imagine the wind in your face. Let's make a right bank. Rotate your right palm down in the front; rotate your left palm up in the front. Lean to your right. You just moved your "ailerons" so that you could make a right turn.

The last control surface is the rudder. It looks like the rudder on a boat, but on an airplane the rudder has a different purpose. The main use of the rudder on an airplane is to make it go straight through the air.

When you look at our little airplane below, you see that we have two engines. Imagine only one of those engines, the one on the right side, producing thrust. In this case, the airplane would want to turn in the direction opposite of the right engine producing thrust, or to the left. This is called "yaw." So, we would then need to deflect the rudder to the right to counter the nose of the airplane yawing to the left to make it fly straight.

The main purpose of the rudder on an airplane is during times when one of the engines is not producing thrust and that is a rare occasion so we don't use the rudder that much. Yaw is controlled by a pilot's feet pushing on rudder pedals.

Look at the figure below and see the various control surfaces.

The engine power is controlled using the throttle. Pushing the throttle increases power; pulling the throttle decreases power.

Imagine that you're now on the runway and you want to fly off the runway. You push the throttles forward, which is like the gas pedal of the car, and you make the airplane go faster.

At a predefined speed based on how much we weigh, we pull back on the control column, which makes the elevator deflect up, causing the air to push the tail down. Then the nose pitches up, and we fly off of the runway.

What if we want to stop for any reason once we've started our takeoff roll? We simply reduce the thrust levers to idle and apply brakes like you would on a car.

Braking is accomplished by pushing on the top of the rudder pedals. These brakes are used only when the plane is on the ground to slow it down or to prepare for stopping.

KEY TAKEAWAYS

- Airplanes fly by moving through the air. The faster we go, the "thicker" the air feels.

- Besides the main wings, there are a lot of "mini-wings" that use the same aerodynamic forces in conjunction with the cockpit controls together allowing the pilot to control the airplane.

- When we are flying, lift always opposes weight, and thrust is always opposite drag. All forces are in balance.

CHAPTER 7

WHY IS FLYING SO SAFE?

"Your flight may be the safest part of your day."

—CAPT RON

Fact:

Consider this: "In 2017 there were 1,000 fatal car crashes in Arizona. In 2017 alone, the National Safety Council estimated 40,000 people across the country died in car accidents. Compare that with the fact that the Aviation Safety Network says 2017 was the safest year ever in aviation."

If you were a frequent flyer, you may have heard the legend of the pilot who bid passengers farewell after landing with these words: "The safest part of your trip is now over." This isn't just one pilot's boast. It's a truth most air travelers take for granted.

Next time you climb into a taxi or an Uber to make the trip from the airport to your destination, consider this:

- What do you know about the driver in whose hands you have placed your life?
- How well has the car been maintained?
- Look out the window—are all the signal lights working?

- Is the road in good shape?
- What about the other motorists?
- Where did they learn to drive?
- How conscientious have those other drivers been about getting enough sleep and avoiding alcohol?

Safety is an accumulation of knowledge about risk converted into practice, and no other mode of transportation has been as expansive as flying in incorporating what we know about the fallibility of humans and machines. As a result, the act of hurtling through the air at 500 mph, six miles above the ground, is less likely to result in your demise than almost any other type of travel. From the plane seats to the cabin air to the course and altitude of the flight, every decision in commercial aviation comes after careful consideration of its impact on safety.

Here are three key factors and how they contribute to why flying is so safe:

1. Technology
2. Air Traffic Control
3. Study of Human Factors

1 - TECHNOLOGY

Here are the key areas of technology that help to make aviation safe:

Jet Engine Technology:

The desire to get faster from A to B as well as economics played a key role in driving the innovation of jet engine propulsion technology.

Jet engines in service today are highly efficient and super reliable. What do I mean by highly efficient? If you would want to make an engine better than an engine that you already have, what would make it better? The first thing you'd want to do to make the engine better would be to make it lighter and produce more thrust. Engines used to weigh something like 10,000 to 15,000 pounds. So, if you could make one that was half as heavy but twice as powerful, that would be a good place to start.

And this is exactly what happened in my career. Jet engines now weigh half as much as they used to, and they produce twice as much thrust and burn less fuel.

When commercial aviation transitioned from propellers to jet engines, wing sweep was introduced as well. A swept wing is a wing that angles backward from its root rather than in a straight sideways direction.

As the jet aircraft were flying at increased speeds, turbulence and drag increased as well due to air friction on the wings.

To demonstrate this for yourself, slowly move your hand through water. You will notice that the water passes over it softly. Now, increase the speed with which you are moving your hand through the water. The result is the you will see and feel turbulence and disturbances in the water. The same principle holds true when an airliner moves from slow speed to high speed.

Swept wing technology was introduced to solve this instability and vibration in jet airplanes at high speed.

Students often ask me about the winglets on the tips of the wings.
When airflow around the wingtips streams out behind the airplane, a vortex is formed. Winglets were created to reduce those wingtip vortices which occur due to the difference between the pressure on the upper surface of an airplane's wing and that on the lower surface.

According to Boeing, winglets installed on its 757 and 767 airliners can improve fuel burn by 5% and cut CO_2 emissions by up to 5%.

Winglet Performance

Regular Wing Tip   with Winglet

Then We Started Stretching the Airplanes.

We keep the same basic design and don't have to go back to the drawing board for a redesign. Just stretch the airplane a little bit and put some more people in it.

TCAS - Traffic Collision and Avoidance System.

That helps us keep away from other airplanes. TCAS works by sending out signals to another aircraft's transponders. The transponder will reply to the signal much in the same way it responds to radar. From the time difference between the interrogation and the reply, the distance to the other aircraft is calculated. The reply signal itself also includes the altitude of that airplane.

Metallurgy

This includes the metals and the actual materials that we use to build airplanes.

For example, the Boeing 787, which is a long-range, midsize wide-body, twin-engine jet airliner that can seat 242–335 passengers, is the world's first major commercial airliner to use composite materials as the primary material in its airframe.

According to Boeing, each Boeing 787 aircraft contains approximately 32,000 kg of CFRP composites, made with 23 tons of carbon fiber. Composites are used on the fuselage, wings, tail, doors and interior. This makes the aircraft not only stronger and more resilient but also more fuel efficient.

Wind Shear Alert Systems

These systems are used for operating in areas where there are thunderstorms. The advent of wind shear alert systems followed an accident at New York's JFK airport in 1975.

At that time, the Eastern Airlines flight EA66 became the deadliest single-aircraft crash in U.S. history. It also sparked the FAA to develop the first Low Level Wind Shear Alert System (LLWAS). Its purpose is to detect large scale wind shifts, such as sea breeze fronts, gust fronts and cold and warm fronts.

Navigation Systems Automation in The Cockpit

Air navigation differs from the navigation of surface craft in several ways. Because aircraft travel at relatively high speeds, there is less time to calculate their position en route. This is why commercial aircraft are fitted with a variety of navigation aids. These are Automatic Direction Finder (ADF), inertial navigation, compasses, radar navigation, VHF omnidirectional range (VOR) and Global Navigation Satellite System (GNSS). The use of GNSS in aircraft has become increasingly common because GNSS provides very precise aircraft position, altitude, heading and ground speed information. GNSS has a standard 5-meter location accuracy worldwide, 24 hours a day, in all weather. If even better accuracy is required, differential techniques are available to provide decimeter or even centimeter accuracy.

* * *

2 - AIR TRAFFIC CONTROL (ATC)

Air traffic control has changed tremendously during my lifetime, going from basically a non-radar environment to having almost all of the United States under constant radar and soon-to-be constant satellite observation.

Basically, the use of radar and computerization has automated a lot of things. In the old days, a controller had a raw return, just the read outs shouting out a beam of energy that bounced back and told the controller how far away the plane was. Then when I was a student pilot, air traffic control advanced to altitude report, altitude and coding.

Eventually the system evolved so that now the controller not only knew where I was located in the sky, but they knew my altitude, which was critical. Before this advancement, controllers could only see two blips on the same part of the target, and unless they knew that the planes were at different altitudes, they had to worry about collision.

With the advent of computerization, controllers see a little data flag around every airplane and it identifies the call sign, what airline, what altitude it is, and what the ground speed is.

The system is constantly analyzing, through vector analysis, to make sure that it's not the two targets or not colliding on a collision course like that. In addition, we have TCAS, the traffic collision avoidance system.

Let's say there is another airplane that's climbing up and I happen to be in cruise. The TCAS will analyze both of our signals. If it senses that we might be coming close to each other, it will inform the other pilot and me and provide both of us with a resolution.

The global navigation satellite systems (GNSS) benefits commercial aviation by aiding aircraft to fly directly from departure to destination, using the most fuel-efficient routes. GNSS allows navigation of difficult terrain at low altitude. This satellite navigation provides us the flexibility to design new procedures that enable planes to fly closer together to increase the arrival and departure rates. Additionally, it enables continuous climb and descent operations to minimize fuel consumption, noise, and carbon emissions.

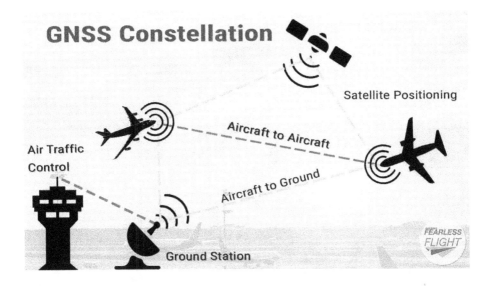

Specifically, the Automatic Dependent Surveillance-Broadcast (ADS-B) is going to be a key element of future air traffic management.

Unlike the current surveillance system, where a ground-based radar transmits "outgoing" signals and uses the "replies" from aircraft transponders to determine location, ADS-B equipped aircraft broadcast their GNSS positions once per second. The information received by air traffic controllers, and other ADS-B aircraft, includes the aircraft's identification, altitude, speed, velocity, projected path and other useful information. It is not dependent upon ground base radar stations which aren't available over the oceans.

However, its widespread implementation is not anticipated until sometime between 2020 and 2025 due to the cost of retrofitting planes with ADS-B.

So just how accurate is the global navigation satellite system?

Well, consider this the next time you are sitting on an airplane heading to your Europe vacation.

The North Atlantic Organized Track System (NAT)

Each day, over 2,000 aircraft travel across the Atlantic Ocean destined for North America or Europe on the North Atlantic Organized Track System.

VIDEO

Watch this impressive 2-Minute visualisation of the airplane traffic on the NAT system in a 24hr period.

http://flf.link/BKBONUS-NATS-24hr

Because most passengers want to fly this route, Europe bound 8pm and 3am ET, and North America bound between 7am to 3pm ET, all aircraft have to select a track, or route.

To accommodate these high-volume traffic times air traffic planners in Gander, Newfoundland and Prestwick, Scotland create weather optimized routes across the Atlantic, called the North Atlantic Organized Track system (NAT).

Think of NAT as a multi-lane, interstate highway in the sky.

To provide the most efficient routes for the airlines these tracks are recalculated daily and published online. Airline dispatchers and pilots use the published tracks to plan the day's flights.

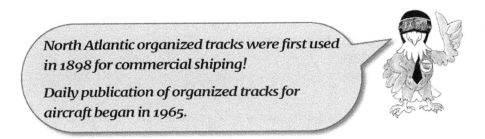

North Atlantic organized tracks were first used in 1898 for commercial shiping!

Daily publication of organized tracks for aircraft began in 1965.

Even though controllers do not have radar coverage over the Atlantic Ocean, they still must ensure all the aircraft are safely separated by distance and altitude. Since they can't "see" the aircraft, controllers rely on us pilots to report our position at regular intervals.

Our position report includes the aircraft's location, speed, and altitude so the controller can build a 3-dimensional model of all the traffic. In the old days, we reported our position by HF radio every 10° longitude. Now it's digital (and much easier).

We will take a closer look at Airport Traffic Control in the next chapter as well.

✳ ✳ ✳

3 - HUMAN FACTORS

The last one is the study of human factors. Human Factors can be defined as the link between knowledge, the environment in which we work, personal circumstances, and communication between team members.

For as long as there have been airplanes, there have been people who uphold and execute their safe operation. Historically, the focus of aircraft maintenance and pilot performance has been on the machinery and skills.

However, good pilots, aircraft mechanics, etc. are much more than the sum of the skills.

Human factors training is assisting aviation departments in analyzing and optimizing the physical and psychological traits we all possess, which define working relationships and job performance.

The objective of the human factors training is to examine the human role in the chain of events that cause an aviation occurrence, and to develop ways to prevent or lessen the seriousness of the occurrence.

Nowadays, in the Western World, most accidents and untoward outcomes are rarely due to lack of resources. They are more likely due to human factors.

One of the reasons accidents happen, even though it's the safest way to fly, is because of human interaction. In fact, pilot error is the leading cause of commercial airline accidents, with close to 80% percent of accidents caused by pilot error, according to Boeing. The other 20% are mainly due to faulty equipment and unsafe, weather-related flying conditions.

The airline industry has some good pilots, terrific pilots in most cases. But on the other side when it comes to interacting and sharing information, it makes it problematic for them. That is one of the reasons though that aviation has gotten even safer in the last 15 to 20 years. The Human Factors Program.

It identifies human behavior in a group that cause problems with communicating with each other. So how did the human factors program in aviation come about? Our human factors program is now being looked at by the medical community who are now implementing some of the practices that we do in aviation to improve patient care and reducing patient mistakes.

According to a recent study by Johns Hopkins, more than 250,000 people in the United States die every year because of medical mistakes, making it the third leading cause of death after heart disease and cancer. Other reports claim the numbers to be as high as 440,000.

One key reason is that self-reporting of minor incidents, which is a cornerstone that makes aviation safer every year, is not widely embraced in the medical community due to liability and potential lawsuits.

KEY TAKEAWAYS

- Commercial Aviation is safe due to Three Factors:
  1. Ongoing Technology Improvements
  2. Air Traffic Control
  3. The Study of Human Factors

- Next time you are quaking in your boots at 40,000 feet, take some comfort knowing you are much safer up there than driving to and from the airport.

CHAPTER 8

THE 8 CRITICAL ELEMENTS OF AIRWORTHINESS

*"It ain't Orville and Wilbur's airplane anymore; times
have changed and so have airplanes."*

—CAPT RON

What Do We Mean By "Airworthiness?"

Airworthiness is the measure of an aircraft's suitability for safe flight. Certification of airworthiness is conferred by a certificate of airworthiness from the state of aircraft registry national aviation authority and is maintained by performing the required maintenance actions.

Who Is Responsible for the Airworthiness of An Aircraft?

While the owner or operator is primarily responsible by this rule it does not relieve the pilot from the responsibility of determining the airworthiness of the aircraft prior to and during a flight or a mechanic from performing airworthy repairs.

To be ready to fly on an airplane, a person needs to understand and fully embrace the 9 critical elements of airworthiness.

What Are Those Elements?

The 8 Critical Elements of Airworthiness

1. Aircraft Design and Development
2. Air Traffic & Airport Control
3. Pilot Training
4. Mechanical Engineers
5. Flight Attendants
6. Aircraft Maintenance
7. Flight Operations

1 - AIRCRAFT DESIGN AND DEVELOPMENT

In the past 48 years, the world's commercial airliners powered by CFM56 aircraft engines have racked up over one billion flight hours. The airline industry has been using the steady stream of data and information to constantly improve the design of airplanes and engines.

Modern design and development of airplanes are completed using computer modeling. This was not always the case; however, it has made for much safer practices for pilots, and ultimately for the passengers of airplanes.

In 1995, the first aircraft was produced through computer-aided design and engineering. Boeing debuted the twin-engine 777, the biggest two-engine jet ever to fly and the first aircraft produced through computer-aided design and engineering. Only a nose mockup was actually built before the vehicle was assembled—and the assembly was only 0.03 mm out of alignment when a wing was attached.

The traditional mechanical controls have increasingly been replaced by electronic ones. So-called fly-by-wire aircraft includes the Airbus A330, A340 and A380 as well as the Boeing 777 and the 787.

The flight controls and displays feature multipurpose designs, are highly efficient and are continually tested to make sure they provide necessary information in an easy-to-see, easy-to-operate manner. The size, shape, placement and appearance of every control, light, switch and feature has been planned and designed in such a way that they are visible in all light conditions.

Additionally, as pilots we need to know that when we have made an input, the system has received it. In case of an error, we need to get feedback. Flight-deck engineers are constantly observing pilots in simulators to improve the ideal reach of controls, the displays are always visible and the seats comfortable for extended periods of time.

In the cabin of the aircraft, safety is the most important design factor as well. You may be complaining, and rightfully so, about the lack of leg room in economy but did you know that a modern airliner seat is designed to withstand 16 times the force of gravity?

All airplane seats meet tough standards for durability and head-impact protection. The fabrics and cushions are fire retardant and self-extinguishing. They are designed not to emit toxic fumes.

As you can imagine by now, even the items you find in the seat pockets are tested to make sure they can't become deadly. Any insulation in the cabin is fire retardant, and, in the case of a fire, emergency lighting is close to the floor. As the flight attendants point out to us in their pre-flight safety briefing, this makes it easier to locate the exits in a smoke-filled cabin.

Most safety standards that are enforced today, like being able to get all passengers off a plane in an emergency within 90 seconds and with decreased accessibility, are due to accidents that have happened in the past. There are many measures put in place to prevent accidents from ever occurring again.

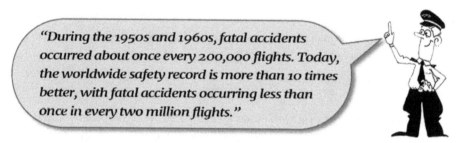

"During the 1950s and 1960s, fatal accidents occurred about once every 200,000 flights. Today, the worldwide safety record is more than 10 times better, with fatal accidents occurring less than once in every two million flights."

The key piece of information to remember about aircraft design is that most commercial aviation accidents are not fatal. Of the 300+ accidents, worldwide, since 2005, less than 25% involved fatalities.

* * *

2 - AIR TRAFFIC AND AIRPORT CONTROL

Just like in the Wizard of Oz, the real magicians of modern day Air Worthiness is the high-tech air traffic system where airplanes guided by GPS will fly self-programmed routes, communicating with each other and with the ground. This is very different from my early days in the air force when maps, blackboards and pencil and paper calculations were used to direct airplanes.

With more than 34 million total flight departures worldwide in 2016, it takes a pretty sophisticated process to safely and efficiently manage a huge—and still growing—number of aircraft.

Every day, the FAA's Air Traffic Organization (ATO) provides service to more than 42,000 flights and 2.5 million airline passengers across more than 29 million square miles of airspace.

In 2014 alone air carriers operating in U.S. airspace transported 871.8 million passengers. Connecting onboard and on-the-ground systems allowed us to create the equivalent of interstate highways in the sky where nobody veers out of their lanes. Hazards that could threaten to close airports and divert airplanes, such as challenging terrain, low visibility or bad weather have been mitigated through improved technology and training.

Airport Control

More noticeably, profound innovations in safety can be seen right here at airports across the country. Motion-detection monitors show every vehicle on every runway, taxiway and terminal gate. Airport controllers are alerted to potential collisions. The reduction of risk improves safety, and this is what the main driving factor is and the reason no other mode of transportation is as safe as commercial aviation.

If you have flown on a commercial airline before, there is a good chance that you may have experienced circling your destination airport in a holding pattern before being cleared to land.

Anxious flyers always want to know that if congestion occurs, wouldn't it be smarter to hold planes BEFORE they take off (or somewhere mid-route) instead of having planes flying in circles like vultures near the congested airport?

The reason this often comes up for fearful flyers is that when they hear the captain come on and letting them know that they are on final approach to their destination, they finally relax, knowing the ordeal is over in about 20 minutes. If something unexpected happens, like the plane being put into a holding pattern, in the absence of knowledge, the mental dialogue starts going into overdrive.

So, if you ever should be on a plane that's being placed into a holding pattern, here is what you need to know to give your rider what it needs to help you regulate and replace your debilitating mental dialogue with a more empowering one.

All Airports have their own 'capacity' numbers in terms of just how many arrivals and departures can safely be handled there per hour, with little to no delay.

This Airport capacity is based on several factors such as:

- Number of runways
- Length of runways
- Weather conditions
- Available instrument approaches
- and more

Arrival and departure volume may be reduced by events such as a runway closure. Other capacity limiting factors include adverse weather conditions, aircraft accidents, inoperative landing aids, equipment failures within the controlling air traffic facility, etc.

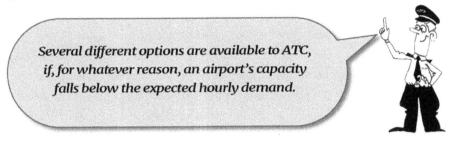

Several different options are available to ATC, if, for whatever reason, an airport's capacity falls below the expected hourly demand.

In fact, there are people responsible to monitor airport capacity and make necessary alterations to deal with the demand.

One relatively simple way to control arrival demand on an airport is by implementing what is called 'mile-in-trail' (MIT) restrictions. When MIT is used for a certain airport, air traffic facilities are advised to space their departures headed for that airport more widely than usual. Twenty miles in trail is a common restriction. MIT aims to provide controllers at the arrival end with a manageable flow that won't exceed the airport's limited capacity.

If, for example, arrival capacity is reduced at New York's JFK due to heavy snow and closed runways, a Ground-delay Program (GDP) may be implemented. Essentially, a GDP adjusts the expected departure times of flights headed for JFK.

These flights take their delay at the departure point. Without the GDP, they'd take off at their originally scheduled times and fly to the New York area, where many would end up in holding patterns because the airborne demand exceeded JFK's current arrival capacity.

If things get especially bad at the arrival airport, ATC has one ace up their sleeve. A Ground Stop. If a Ground Stop is executed for a particular airport – all flights destined for that airport must remain at their point of departure until the Ground Stop is lifted.

These measures were devised to keep the air-traffic system from becoming overwhelmed by airplanes with no place to go but the holding patterns.

Still, as old and inefficient as they are, holding patterns remain an inevitability. Unforeseen, short term constraints at the destination airport may require some limited airborne holding. One instance would be when an ATC needs to change landing direction at an airport. The planes closest to the destination might have to be delayed until the switchover is complete. Holding patterns works well in such cases.

* * *

Another question we often address frequently on our weekly **FearlessFlight® LIVE Show** is:

"Who Has the Ultimate Decision-Making Authority In An Emergency? Is It Air Traffic Control or The Pilot?

As mentioned before, controllers generally are responsible for preventing collisions as well as organizing and expediting the flows of traffic. For controllers to achieve these objectives, we pilots must, by law, comply with ATC instructions.

However; if an emergency occurs on board my aircraft, I am authorized and responsible to do whatever necessary to mitigate the situation. In this case, it is the controllers who must ensure to provide any assistance they can under the circumstances. This could mean diverting or rerouting other flights.

Another way to think of it is this. If you must stop where a sign is posted that says "No Stopping" because your car is on fire; you'll stop. The police and emergency responders will do whatever they can to assist; even if it means redirecting traffic around you.

* * *

3 - PILOT TRAINING

Modern era pilots have become the general managers of information, and technology plays the part of the heavy-hitter role on the flight deck. However, as Captain "Sully" Chesley Sullenberger has so aptly demonstrated on January 15, 2009, technology is no substitute for experience, skill and good judgment. Sully and his first officer, Jeff Skiles, successfully landed their Airbus A320 US Airways Flight 1549 on the Hudson River in New York.

For a pilot to be considered an applicant for a pilot for a major airline, they need to have at least 3,500 to 4,500 hours of experience. That's about 146-188 days (24 hours) of straight flying! It could also be considered in terms of an 8-hour working day, which would be about 438-563 days.

This means, it would take a pilot, at least a year and a half of flying every day for 8 hours, minimum, before they would even be considered. That's a lot of training!

Their training is even more specific than that with some needing to be completed in a turbo jet or turbo prop plane. Each pilot is typically only certified to one airplane type, being that it is so expensive and time consuming to certify a pilot. Much of that training is done using simulators that cover all scenarios and prepare a pilot for anything that could happen. Pilot recurrent training happens approximately every 9 months and requires that a pilot prove their competency. If they are unable to, there are sent to be retrained within a certain period. Essentially, if a pilot is unable to prove they are competent, they will lose their job.

A supervisory pilot flies with the pilot until satisfied the pilot can operate independently.

> *Capt Eric and I met many years ago when he was assigned to me as my first officer. A lifelong friendship developed and Capt Eric now volunteers his time and expertise at our classes in Phoenix and Los Angeles.*

Pilots always fly with another pilot who can report performance problems to supervisors. As a matter of fact, Eric and I met many years ago when he was assigned to me as my first officer. A lifelong friendship developed and Capt Eric now volunteers his time and expertise at our classes in Phoenix and Los Angeles. At the time this book was first published, Capt Eric is still on active duty roster and piloting a Boeing 757.

Pilots are tested for alcohol and drug use without warning.

A FAA check pilot or a company check pilot can observe a pilot's performance on any flight without advance warning.

Pilots must pass a medical assessment ensuring they are fit to fly (reduces to every 6 months above a certain age).

Pilots must also complete a 'Line Check.' This is a bit like a driving test, but in the aircraft. An examiner observes us operating the aircraft to ensure we are compliant with company rules and regulations and are doing the job to a proficient standard.

Every 6 months, pilots must go into the simulator where we practice emergency procedures whilst being assessed by an examiner over a couple of days. They also complete technical testing to ensure they maintain a high level of technical proficiency on their aircraft type.

All pilots are required to complete Crew Resource Management (CRM) Training. This is where pilots are taught about how human factors can affect flight safety.

* * *

4 - MECHANICAL ENGINEERS

Mechanics, like pilots, need to be certified. This requires extensive training and an apprenticeship, no matter their previous experience, for a mechanic to work alone. In the US, every mechanic must be certified by the Federal Aviation Administration (FAA). There are several different specialized types of aircraft mechanic. Any aircraft mechanic is trained to handle pre-flight inspections, check-ups and general maintenance.

Aviation Maintenance Technical Engineer (AMTE)

The responsibility of an aviation maintenance technical engineer primarily rests on the interrelated parts of an aircraft and how performance issues in one area can impact others. They are aware of the subtlest changes in how parts operate. These technicians also recommend design changes and improvements based on the data they gather and experience.

Avionics Technician

Capt Eric, who pilots a Boeing 747 told me once that his plane carries more than 150 miles of wires onboard. To make sure no wires are crossed, avionics technicians are responsible for the wiring and electrical systems aboard an aircraft, including the complex electronic instruments. Their focus lies in ensuring adequate power supply to all systems as well as calibrating and correcting our instruments.

Advanced Structures Technician

When it comes to the maintenance and repair of a great variety of different large aircraft structures, especially those structures that are impacted by atmospheric conditions in flight, we need this type of technician. They are both knowledgeable about aircraft maintenance and are familiar with sheet metal, metal composites, and metallurgy.

Of course, there are also the mechanics who are working in the hangars, specializing in the air frame or engine overhauls, and those who work on the line directing the plane and maintaining them before their next flight.

* * *

5 - FLIGHT ATTENDANTS

Contrary to popular belief, a flight attendant's primary concern is not getting the passengers their coffee and snacks. Their primary concern is safety. Flight attendants are highly trained to do their jobs...which they do with a smile on their face!

When you come to one of our classes, you might meet one of our long-standing volunteers, and good friend of mine, Diane Hansen.

Diane has volunteered for nearly 15 years as a Navigator at Phoenix Sky Harbor International Airport.

At the tender age of 70, Diane decided to realize her high school dream, and became a Flight Attendant. At the time, I am writing this book, she is still actively flying, and would tell you that Flight Attendant training is not for the faint-hearted.

The training to become a flight attendant is comprehensive and, first and foremost, covers safety and security procedures, and first aid. Of course, customer service, pre-flight procedures, boarding, and in-flight service are part of the training. Other aspects include the types of planes on which they will be working, how to deal with unruly passengers, and what to do in different kinds of emergency situations.

This training is hands-on, utilizing aircraft simulators and mock-ups. Written and competency exams are an almost daily part of the training; practical tests on emergency procedures must be passed with a score of 100%. Recurrent training is mandatory every 12 months, so their knowledge is refreshed frequently.

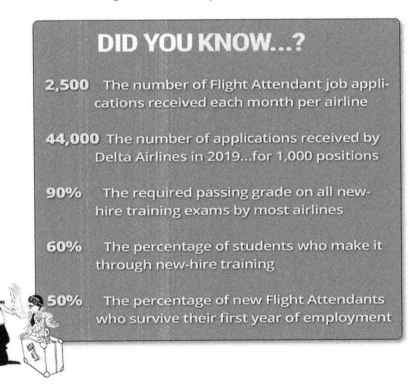

DID YOU KNOW...?

2,500 The number of Flight Attendant job applications received each month per airline

44,000 The number of applications received by Delta Airlines in 2019...for 1,000 positions

90% The required passing grade on all new-hire training exams by most airlines

60% The percentage of students who make it through new-hire training

50% The percentage of new Flight Attendants who survive their first year of employment

Flight Attendants receive on-the-job training from their employer and must be certified by the Federal Aviation Administration (FAA). Since 2004, any flight attendant who works on an aircraft with more than 20 seats must hold a Certificate of Demonstrated Proficiency issued by the FAA.

Flight attendants must successfully pass a FAA approved program which includes training on how to deal with fire prevention and control, the use of emergency equipment, aircraft evacuation and escape, and survival skills for various kinds of crash circumstances.

Because the airlines have high standards and demanding requirements of their flight attendants the following numbers may both comfort and surprise you.

So, the next time you are greeted by your Flight Attendants, you can take comfort in the fact that they underwent a very competitive and rigorous process to have earned their place on the airplane!

* * *

6 - AIRCRAFT MAINTENANCE

Airlines have among the strongest programs of preventative maintenance out there.

The average flight length for a short-haul jet is about 2 hours, whereas a long-haul airliner is around 6-7 hours.

Now as to how many times an aircraft flies, we can find their aircraft design cycle limit in this Federal Register document.

For a 'typical' airliner we can say it is built to average about 40,000 cycles in its lifetime. A cycle constitutes one takeoff and landing. To be more specific, it includes engine start, climb, cruise, landing and shutdown.

Another factor is the average retirement age for a commercial airliner, which is around 24-25 years.

So, In Summary We Have:

- 2 hours/flight
- 40,000 cycles (~20,000 flights)
- 25 years

A typical short-haul jet therefore logs approximately 40,000 flight hours over its 25 years (219,000 hours) of active service. This means for every 1 hour in flight, this aircraft spends on average about 5 hours on the ground.

Obviously, these numbers will vary widely, but for a general reference, that's a very good estimate.

This represents a significant commitment for airlines. Each airplane has a logbook, which has the signature of a certified mechanic verifying the plane's airworthiness. Scheduled maintenance tasks are grouped into work packages known as blocks. The complete package is sometimes referred to as a complete overhaul cycle. The concept is called block maintenance or sometimes progressive maintenance.

Daily Check

This check is the lowest scheduled check. A daily check is a cursory inspection of the aircraft to look for obvious damage and deterioration. It checks for "general condition and security" and reviews the aircraft log for discrepancies and corrective action. The accomplishment of the daily check requires little in the way of specific equipment, tools, or facilities.

A basic requirement is that the airplane remains airworthy. Usually, a daily check is accomplished every 24 to 60 hours of accumulated flight time.

'A' Check

This is the next higher level of scheduled maintenance. It is normally accomplished at a designated maintenance station in the route structure and includes the opening of access panels to check and service certain items.

The actual rate that this check is performed, varies by aircraft type, the cycle count, or the number of hours flown since the last check. In general, an 'A' check is performed every 400-600 flight hours or 200–300 cycles, depending on aircraft type.

Remember that one takeoff and one landing is considered one aircraft "cycle." While an 'A' check can be completed in 10-15 hours of the plane being on the ground, the actual man-hours are about 50-70 hours.

'B' Check

This is a slightly more detailed check of components and systems. It is performed approximately every 6-8 months. It needs about 160-180 man-hours, depending on the aircraft, and is usually completed within 1–3 days at an airport hangar.

Special equipment and tests are required. It does not involve, however, detailed disassembly or removal of components.

While the label 'B' check still exists, most contemporary maintenance programs do not use the 'B' check interval. Instead, the tasks which were originally defined for this interval have, for many airplanes, been distributed between the 'A' and 'C' check.

'C' Check

This is a major check of individual systems and components for serviceability and function. This check puts the aircraft out of service, and the aircraft must not leave the maintenance site until it is completed. In terms of frequency and time to completion, 'C' checks depend on many factors. Generally, they are performed either:

- every 20–24 months or a specific amount of actual flight hours (or cycles)

  or

- as required by the manufacturer

A 'C' check requires a thorough visual inspection of specified areas, components and systems as well as operational or functional checks. It is an advanced check that involves extensive tooling, test equipment, and special skill levels. The 'C' check includes the lower checks, i.e. 'A,' 'B,' and Daily checks.

As you can imagine, this is a heavy maintenance procedure and the time needed to complete such a check is at least 7-14 days. The effort involved can require up to 6,000 man-hours!

'D' Check

A 'D' check is the most in-depth and requires that the airplane is basically taken apart for inspection and overhaul and put back together. It is also referred to as the "Structural Check." It includes detailed visual and other non-destructive test inspections of the aircraft structure. It is an intense inspection of the structure for evidence of corrosion, structural deformation, cracking, and other signs of deterioration or distress and involves extensive disassembly to gain access for inspection.

Like your doctor, mechanics use X-ray and ultrasound machines for this testing. This check occurs approximately every six years. In certain circumstances where further inspection on the fuselage skin is required, even the paint may need to be completely removed. Depending on the aircraft and the number of technicians involved, a 'D' check can generally take up to 50,000 man-hours and up to 60 days or longer to complete.

As you probably have guessed, this is by far the most expensive testing procedure and on average the costs for a single 'D' check is in the million-dollar range. A commercial airplane receives three D checks before being retired.

This is how airplanes can last well over 20 years and still be fit to fly.

Many airlines use a scheduled 'D' check also as an opportunity to make major cabin modifications on the aircraft which may include new seats, entertainment systems, carpeting, etc.

Many fearful flyers are very concerned about the safety of the aircraft. It is true that in favor of reducing the (labor) costs of these maintenance procedures, US Airways and Southwest fly planes to a maintenance facility in El Salvador for their 'C' and 'D' checks. Delta sends planes to Mexico. United uses a facility in China.

After the merger with US-Airways, American Airlines has begun outsourcing their heavy maintenance to Hong Kong.

The company they contract, HAECO, has been in business since 1950 and has been recognized for its MRO (Maintenance, Repair, Overhaul) services. The company is owned by Swire – the parent company of Cathay Pacific and maintains aircraft of many other major airlines around the world.

While, of course, it is unfortunate that jobs are lost here in the US, I do want to make clear just how safe flying in the US really is.

Data from the National Highway Traffic Safety Administration shows that in 2017, fatal motor vehicle accidents caused 37,133 deaths. That comes out to be 1.16 fatalities per 100 million vehicle miles traveled, and nearly 12 people for every 100,000 U.S. residents.

Contrast the above numbers with those of the Aviation Safety Network (ASN). In 2018, it recorded a total of 15 fatal commercial airliner accidents, leading to 556 deaths. Compare this with only 10 accidents and 44 lives lost in 2017, the safest year in aviation history. A Dutch Aviation Consultancy calculated a rate of one fatal accident for every 3 million flights, based on the 2018 data available.

And of course, as you know, one of the crashes was the Lion Air flight JT610 involved the now infamous new Boeing 737 MAX aircraft.

To go into detail about the causes and circumstances that led to that crash, as well as Ethiopian flight ET302 is beyond the scope of this book.

My heart goes out to the victims, their families and relatives. And while the grieving is a necessary part of the process, so is learning from our mistakes. And this is one area where the airline industry shines, and the main reason aviation is the safest means of transportation by far.

* * *

This brings me to what I call the concept of **Necessary Fallibility in Aviation**.

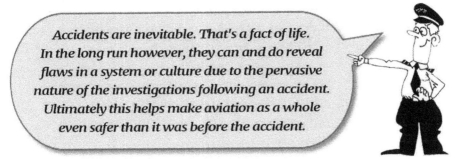

Accidents are inevitable. That's a fact of life. In the long run however, they can and do reveal flaws in a system or culture due to the pervasive nature of the investigations following an accident. Ultimately this helps make aviation as a whole even safer than it was before the accident.

What this means for the Boeing 737 MAX is that it will be the safest aircraft type on the planet when all investigations, modifications and certifications are completed.

I also have empathy for those who would say that this isn't very comforting to the victims and their families. And while tragic, this crash, or any other commercial aviation incident, is not a confirmation for continuing to justify your fear of flying. To put it in my own words:

The pain in your brain is not about the plane.

To give you some perspective: As Americans, according to the National Safety Council, we have a 1 in 7 chance of dying from heart disease and cancer. I am sure you agree that these are not good odds.

We have a 1 in 114 chance of dying in a car crash. Slightly better, but still not all that great, considering how much time we spend on the road.

In contrast, the odds of dying in an "Air and Space Transport Incident," which include all manner of private flights, are 1 in 9,821(!)

Now these are very good odds. In fact, these odds are 87(!) times better than your chances perishing in a motor vehicle accident.

I do not want to minimize the very real issues of ensuring sound and transparent certification processes or outsourcing maintenance to other countries in order to save labor costs. I do, however, want to make sure you fully understand that next time you drive to an airport to board a flight, your risk of dying is exponentially greater than boarding that flight.

* * *

7 - FLIGHT OPERATIONS

Non-normal operations are what pilots would consider an "emergency" or "abnormal." To them, it is out of the norm. "Emergencies" do happen, however, the pilots are well trained, and each airplane has a Quick Reference Handbook (QRH) and an Emergency or Abnormal Checklist (EAC), which lists the steps a crew would go through to handle any scenario. Each pilot on a plane, the Captain and First Officer are also trained to handle alternate duties and for normal operation of the airplane. There are flying duties and non-flying duties that are shared.

An emergency situation is a circumstance in which the safety of the aircraft or of persons on board or on the ground is endangered for any reason.

An abnormal situation is defined as a circumstance in which it is no longer possible to continue the flight using normal procedures. The important distinction is that in this situation the safety of the aircraft, crew or passengers on board or on the ground is not in danger.

Many times, the news media reports that tend to trigger anxious flyers paint the picture of an emergency situation, when in fact, it often is an abnormal situation.

The occurrence of one or more factors within or outside an aircraft may escalate into either an abnormal or an emergency situation.

An emergency or abnormal situation may result in it being impossible to continue the flight to a destination as planned, resulting in one or more of the following outcomes:

- Loss of altitude
- Diversion to a nearby airport
- Forced landing

For Example:

Emergency Situations

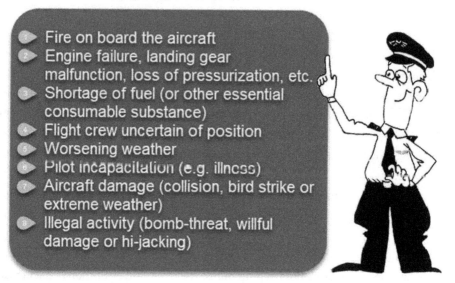

1. Fire on board the aircraft
2. Engine failure, landing gear malfunction, loss of pressurization, etc.
3. Shortage of fuel (or other essential consumable substance)
4. Flight crew uncertain of position
5. Worsening weather
6. Pilot incapacitation (e.g. illness)
7. Aircraft damage (collision, bird strike or extreme weather)
8. Illegal activity (bomb-threat, willful damage or hi-jacking)

Regardless the situation, first, and foremost, a pilot's priority is safety. Nothing that we do is more important than safety because other than the responsibility for the lives on board, at the end of the day, we want to get home to our families too. As the father of two, this was certainly true for me!

The Second priority for a pilot is passenger comfort. As pilots we want you, our passengers, to be able to enjoy flying so you will come back and fly with us again. Job security!

The third priority is scheduling. Safety and comfort come first, even if a flight is behind schedule.

Lastly is efficiency. If all the other priorities are met, fuel economy, operating the airplane, etc. become important.

* * *

8 - REGULATIONS AND COMPLIANCE

As you can imagine by now, there are a great many rules and regulations to be observed and complied with in civil and specifically in commercial aviation. The *Commercial Space Launch Act of 1984* directs the FAA to exercise this responsibility consistent with public health and safety, safety of property, and the national security and foreign policy interests of the United States.

The Federal Aviation Agency regulates the airlines and has adopted safety as its primary responsibility.

Their Mission Statement Is as Follows:

"Our mission is to provide the safest, most efficient aerospace system in the world and our mantra is to improve the safety and efficiency of aviation, while being responsive to our customers and accountable to the public."

The compliance mandate released by the FAA impacts all business functions of the aviation industry - operationally and strategically.

Mandates such as Continuous Analysis and Surveillance require airlines to have a method of measuring effectiveness and performance of maintenance and inspection, and Internal Evaluation Programs for continuous monitoring of internal processes, programs and procedures.

* * *

The FAA is very clear in its directive that only airworthy aircraft should be operated.

Ultimately the Regulation Places Responsibility On Us, The Pilot, By Stating:

"The pilot in command of a civil aircraft is responsible for determining whether that aircraft is in condition for safe flight. The pilot in command shall discontinue the flight when unairworthy mechanical, electrical, or structural conditions occur."

As you can see, all of these elements contribute to the airworthiness of commercial aircraft and guarantee your safety while at an airport or onboard a flight.

KEY TAKEAWAYS

These are the primary reasons that make air travel the safest way to travel in the world:

- Improvements in aircraft design and development
- Air traffic and airport control
- Advances in pilot training
- Highly qualified mechanical engineers
- Superbly trained flight attendants
- Better aircraft maintenance and quality assurance
- Highly coordinated flight operations

CHAPTER 9

TURBULENCE

"Turbulence is not dangerous, just annoying."

—CAPT RON

Why Turbulence Is No Big Deal

It can feel like the scariest part of flying but turbulence is no cause for alarm. Turbulence is a sudden change in airflow that can be caused by a number of factors. The most common cause is turbulent air in the atmosphere. Jet streams trigger sudden changes in wind speed that can rock the plane. Another type is thermal turbulence. It's created by hot rising air usually from cumulus clouds or thunderstorms.

Mechanical turbulence is caused by the landscape. Mountains or tall buildings can distort the wind flow in the sky above them.

Airplanes can also create turbulence. The wings cause wake turbulence as it passes through the air. This can affect planes flying behind one another. It's why planes avoid taking the same flight path on takeoffs and landings.

Pilots and air traffic control do a lot to avoid turbulence. But even when they do run into it, the risk is low. Modern aircraft are built to withstand even severe turbulence. They can quickly rise and fall up to 100 feet. As a result, turbulence hasn't caused an airplane crash in over 40 years.

Turbulence Forecast

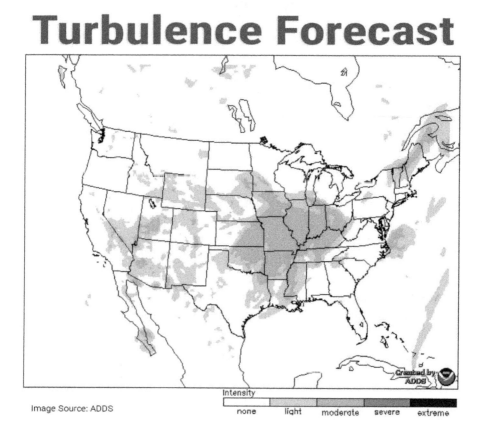

Image Source: ADDS

Intensity

none   light   moderate   severe   extreme

Unfortunately, it has been on the rise. Since 1958, turbulence rose 40-90% over Europe and North America. Studies suggest that global warming could cause it to be worse by 2050.

When booking seats, aim for ones closest to the wings. These will be the smoothest in turbulence.

All turbulence is wind shear, wind shear is the term that the media has connected it with, but it is mostly thunderstorms.

So, whenever you see an article in the paper about thunderstorms, the media is going to talk about wind shear, but wind shear really describes what all turbulence is all about.

So, let me show you with a drawing.

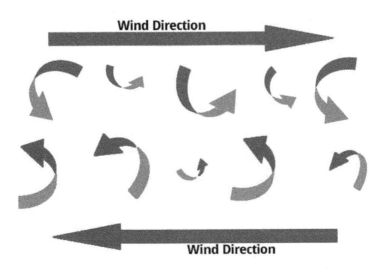

All wind is composed of molecules of air. These molecules are moving in all different directions.

The wind is always circulating. Because it's air, it remains invisible to us. If you were in the water and your had something floating in the water, you can see which way the current is going. But in the air, not so much, especially when you're inside an airplane.

As you can see in the figure, the wind represented by the top arrows moves in one direction. The wind represented by the bottom arrow is moving opposite. Where the two wind currents bump into each other, they create eddies, just like white-water rapids. It is not the eddies, or the turbulence in our case, that create the bumps. It is the fact that we choose to fly through it at 500 mph.

Think of a speed bump in your neighborhood. If you go over the speed bump at 5 mph, it is much less noticeable than if you ride over it at 100 mph. But the laws of physics and aerodynamics frown upon us trying to fly our airplane at 5 mph. And so, the faster we're going, the worse the turbulence is going to seem.

That's turbulence in a nutshell.

* * *

G Force

What is G force? G-force stands for either the force of gravity on a particular extraterrestrial body or the force of acceleration anywhere. It is measured in g's, where 1 g is equal to the force of gravity at the Earth's surface, which is 9.8 meters per second per second.

The G-force on an object is its acceleration relative to free-fall. The object experiences this acceleration due to the vector sum of non-gravitational forces acting per unit of the object's mass. These accelerations, also known as "proper accelerations," are not the result of gravity itself. Because of the stresses and strains on objects, sufficiently large g-forces may result which can be highly destructive to objects and organisms.

It is relevant to us because G-force is what we measure in order to strengthen or to design the airplane to make sure that it's going to withstand what mother nature can throw at us.

So, when you look at that, we're looking at maybe a variation between, let's just say the worst-case scenario would be 1.2 gs to a 1.8, so that would be a down in an updraft on right after another. That's the max you are ever going to see. And then just know that those airplanes that we build out there, they're designed to take like 3 to 4 gs.

So, it's like three to four times what you're ever going to encounter in the airplane. As an example, while you are sitting in the plane, get a bottle of water and put it on your tray table and watch how little the water actually moves up and down. Now take a bottle of water and put it in your car. Now drive over a bumpy road and look at the difference. Compare that in the car to how little it bounced up and down in the air.

And it's going to disrupt your mindset. And that's what it's all about. You know, regardless of how much of a nuisance or how annoying the turbulence is, we know that it is nothing to be afraid of. Our strategy is to disrupt your thinking because it's your thinking that becomes corrupted.

It's not what happens to you, it's what you're thinking about what's happening to you, and so you could just give yourself a break and remind yourself you've got this. You now know that the only lasting effect when it comes to dealing with your anxiety about turbulence, it is to disrupt that thought pattern so that you can get away from the mental, emotional and physical effects of your negative mental dialogue.

So back to wind shear, all turbulence is really a form of wind shear where the molecules of air are bumping along into each other.

* * *

Avoiding Turbulence

Can pilots escape turbulence?

Yes, sometimes it's available to pilots to escape turbulent air masses.

Say we're at 33,000 feet. You notice that everything has been bumping along a little bit and then you notice what sounds like the engines are increased. So that's going to alert you that the pilots are paying attention up there because more than likely what they've done is they've talked to other airplanes in the area that have gone through before us.

So, let's say that one below us reported turbulence and there was another one above us at 35,000 feet but he reported is being smooth. So, what we are going to do is we're going to request from air traffic control to climb to a higher altitude.

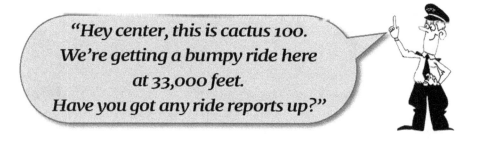

"Hey center, this is cactus 100. We're getting a bumpy ride here at 33,000 feet. Have you got any ride reports up?"

Well, the first thing we're going to do is say, *"Hey center, this is cactus 100. We were getting a bumpy ride here at 33,000 feet. Have you got any ride reports up?"*

The center is going to ask this airplane and this airplane and any other airplanes that are either in the area with us or just passed through the area where we're about to fly through and one of them comes back and says, *"Yeah, we've met a pretty doo ride at 35,000."* He may add similar information saying that it was bumpy before 33,000 feet and they climbed to 35,000 feet and they got out of it.

Well, that's great information because now we know that we have actual pilot reports. It's called Pi Rep and it is in real time. That's why for those of you who look on turbulence.com, save your time because turbulence.com is going to hours old by the time you actually get in the air and in the vicinity of where you have looked at during your preflight planning. And pilots are the ones that are supposed to be doing that anyway. So, don't do their job for them.

So back to the problem here. So, it's been bumpy at 33,000 feet. So, we asked for 35,000 feet, he clears us and then we go up and sure enough it gets smoother. So that's the most common way that we want to find if the ride is better at any other altitudes. And two, it's what we do to communicate constantly about how the rides are. And we can use this when we have thunderstorms in the area, so we can have an airplane that has gone through an area and maybe we're in the clouds and we're looking at radar.

There's nothing showing on the radar, but we're getting a bumpy ride. We can ask the air traffic controller, which way our airplanes deviating up in front of us or people coming through this line. So, we're constantly talking to air traffic control who's constantly talking to all the other airplanes in that area and they're giving us guidance and advice on where the smooth ride is found.

Conversely, let's say that we're flying along at 33,000 feet and you heard the engines noise decrease a little bit. And you were thinking, well, you know, it's about a four-hour flight. We've been doing this for two hours at cruise. So, then you might realize that what's happening is the smoother air is down below you. So, the pilots have requested to move below.

The only reason that we wouldn't be able to instantly climb or descend was if there was another airplane.

If there is another airplane above us going the other way we're going to have to wait until that airplane passes before, we're going to get clearance to go above. So that's one of the best things that we do out there. We're talking constantly.

"If the flight attendant looks worried, that's a sure sign that I need to worry!"

On the one hand, this makes perfect sense—but only if you fall into the trap that this is System 1 or Elephant Brain.

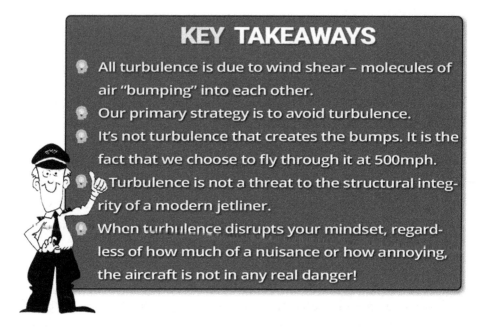

KEY TAKEAWAYS

- All turbulence is due to wind shear – molecules of air "bumping" into each other.
- Our primary strategy is to avoid turbulence.
- It's not turbulence that creates the bumps. It is the fact that we choose to fly through it at 500mph.
- Turbulence is not a threat to the structural integrity of a modern jetliner.
- When turbulence disrupts your mindset, regardless of how much of a nuisance or how annoying, the aircraft is not in any real danger!

When we ask our students which part of their flights, and to what extent, causes them the most stress, about 66% of them mention takeoff and turbulence as the main anxiety producing triggers of their fear of flying.

After 32+ years of working with fearful flyers, I am aware that if turbulence is one of your primary triggers, this chapter may not have held all the answers to satisfy you that indeed your fear of turbulence causing harm to the airplane, or you.

This book focuses on all aspects of your fear of flying. However, my team and I have created a comprehensive 30+ page **Expert Guide to Turbulence and Takeoff**.

The Expert Guide to Turbulence & Takeoffs has been downloaded over 4,368 times!

The PDF Guide is a comprehensive 32 Pages and easy to read. It busts 9 of the most common myths about Takeoffs and Turbulence. It is packed with critical information, strategies and tools that you need to help you get over your fear of takeoffs and turbulence.

Every day we get great feedback and testimonials about the Guide - and we are confident that it will help you in your goal of overcoming your fear of flying.

FREE GUIDE

Two of the most often mentioned triggers are takeoff and Turbulence.

Download your 30-Page Expert Guide to Takeoff and Turbulence today!

http://flf.link/BKBONUS-EGTT

CHAPTER 10

COCKPIT MANAGEMENT

WHAT REALLY GOES ON BEHIND THE COCKPIT DOOR...

"Pilots are the first ones to arrive on the scene of an accident;
That's why WE are totally invested in the
safe outcome of our flight."

—CAPT RON

How Do We Know That We Can Safely Accomplish This Flight?

What you may not realize is that your flight preparation started long before you headed to the airport. Many hours, a lot of personnel and more planning than you can ever imagine has already taken place before you board a commercial airliner. What follows is just a brief introduction, designed to give you an overview.

If after reading this chapter, you have additional questions about what we pilots do to fly safely, join us.

Tuesdays at 6:30 Pacific for your weekly FearlessFlight® LIVE Show

FLIGHT PLANS

Documents [▲ ▼] **EFLIGHT PLAN** FLT 693 03JUN HNL

```
-PHMLU905
-N0463F370 MKK4 EBBER R577 ELKEY DCT JERKI DCT BLH HYDRR1
-KPHX0532 KIWA
-PBN/A1B5C4D4          NAV/RNVD1E2A1 DOF/180604 REG/N201UU
EET/EBBER0036 KZAK0046 KILA0419 SEL/DQGR RALT/PHNL KSFO
RMK/NRP
```

TO / IDENT	LAT / FL	LONG / WIND	MC / NCP	MK / MH	GS / TRR	TD / TAS	SD / I	ST / TLDR	ST / TTLT	SB / TTLB
MOLOKAI	N21082	W157100	094				P11	0044		
MKK	26017	P017	095	031	359	0				
BLUSH	N21200	W156404	057				P09	0030		
BLUSH	28033	P031	054	050	359	0				
TOP OF CLIMB			081		406	P04	0069	0021	0070	
TOC	37 28057	P047	080	000	359	0	2424	0021	0070	
SEEXI	N21171	W154444	081	800	517	P04	0039	0004	0006	
SEEXI	37 28057	P054	081	000	463	0	2385	0025	0076	
ALICA	N21349	W153231	066	800	518	P04	0078	0003	8818	
ALICA	37 28060	P055	063	000	463	0	2307	0034	0088	
EBBER	N21428	W153088	049	800	507	P04	0015	0002	0003	
EBBER	37 28060	P044	044	000	463	0	2292	0036	0091	
ELOYI	N22206	W151531	051	800	509	P02	0080	0010	0013	
ELOYI	37 28060	P047	046	000	462	0	2212	0046	0104	
ERROT	N25165	W145306	051	800	487	M01	0392	0048	0063	
ERROT	37 28014	P027	048	000	460	0	1820	0134	0167	

Documents [▲ ▼] **EFLIGHT PLAN** FLT 693 03JUN HNL

ETNIC	N27547	W138514	053	800	468	P00	0391	0050	0064	
ETNIC	37 27019	P009	052	000	459	0	1429	0224	0231	
ETECO	N30171	W131381	055	800	478	P00	0405	0051	0063	
ETECO	37 21024	P019	055	000	459	0	1024	0315	0294	
EDSEL	N32145	W124059	058	800	477	P01	0404	0051	0062	
EDSEL	37 23016	P017	059	000	460	0	0620	0406	0356	
EDTOO	N32280	W123000	062	800	472	P02	0057	0007	0009	
EDTOO	37 21013	P012	063	000	460	0	0563	0413	0165	
ELKEY	N32410	W122030	061	800	470	P02	0050	0006	0008	
ELKEY	37 22012	P009	062	000	461	0	0513	0419	0373	
JERKI	N33372	W115367	064	800	480	P02	0329	0041	0049	
JERKI	37 24031	P019	066	086	461	0	0184	0500	0422	
BLYTHE	N33357	W114456	078	800	486	P02	0043	0006	0006	
BLH	37 24032	P025	080	045	461	0	0141	0506	0428	
BGN DESCENT			090	800	484	P02	0024	0003	0004	
ROD	37 24034	P023	093	048	461	0	0117		0432	
SCOLE	N33277	W114049	090			P04	0011			
SCOLE	24028	P023	094	048	284	0				
HYDRR	N33164	W113041	090			P15	0052			
HYDRR	23013	P015	093	048	284	0				
GEELA	N33168	W112492	076			P16	0012			
GEELA	21015	P008	077	030	284	0				

Image Source: Capt Eric

Above is a picture of a display that pilots have in their iPads. This is their flight plan track, which is a digital map of where they are, where they are going, and where the various checkpoints that pilots refer to as waypoints are located along the route. A waypoint is an intermediate point or place on a route or line of travel, or a point at which course is changed.

Waypoints are fixes in the flight plan that the pilots are checking fuel and arrival time so that they can see that they are proceeding according to the flight plan, timewise and fuel-wise. The waypoint can be a physical town or fix like Phoenix or Amarillo, or it can be a radio navigation aid or just a point in space. The waypoint always has a five-digit identifier, or five-character identifier made up of letters and numbers.

* * *

Flight Plan Charts

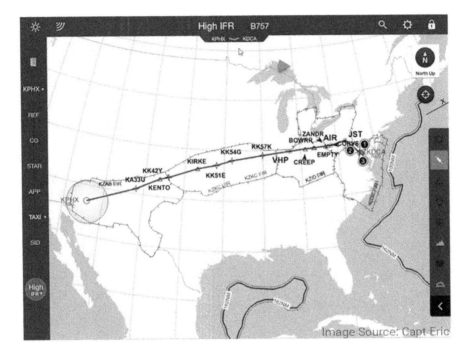

Image Source: Capt Eric

This example depicts a flight plan for a flight from Phoenix to Washington National Airport.

Besides checking time over fixes (waypoints) and checking aircraft fuel burn, we also observe the tracking performance with both the GPS in the airplane and the GPS on the iPad.

We make sure that we are proceeding along the planned route and when we hit every fix, the aircraft establishes itself on course in the direction that we had planned to proceed to the next fix or waypoint.

In the past, we did this in much a different way. We had charts we could monitor, and our flight plan was printed out on a lot of paper that would have all the same information that now exists on the iPad. This was not necessarily like an analog to digital conversion. It was just the way the information was displayed either on paper with charts or in the iPad.

Takeoff Performance

Example:	
OAT	15 °C (59 °F)
Pressure altitude	5,650 feet
Takeoff weight	2,950 lb
Headwind comp.	9.0 knots
Ground roll	1,375 feet
Total distance over a 50 feet obstacle	2,300 feet
Takeoff speed at	
Lift-off	66 knots (76 mph)
50 feet	72 knots (83 mph)

Associated conditions	
Power	Full throttle 2,600 rpm
Mixture	Lean to appropriate fuel pressure
Flaps	Up
Landing gear	Retract after positive climb established
Cowl flaps	Open

Weight pounds	Takeoff speed			
	Lift-off		50 ft	
	kts	MPH	kts	MPH
2,950	66	76	72	83
2,800	64	74	70	81
2,600	63	72	68	78
2,400	61	70	66	76
2,200	58	67	63	73

Next, we are going to review a few things about takeoff performance.

One of the first considerations is:

How Do We Know That the Airplane Will Meet Required Takeoff Distance and Climb Performance?

The previously mentioned dispatch department also runs an analysis of our takeoff performance for any runway we might use at the departure airport. Using the current outside temperature conditions, winds, level of contamination on the runway surface (or no contamination) and aircraft weight, the dispatcher will determine whether we need to use maximum engine thrust or a reduced engine power setting for the planned takeoff. There may be multiple flap settings for all the runways that we might use at a departure airport.

The flap setting for takeoff will be selected based on optimizing takeoff performance for each possible departure runway. The dispatcher considers this and prints a performance section in the body of the flight plan for us to refer to, depending on the runway of intended use.

The performance section of the flight plan will show the airplane number so that we know the takeoff performance was computed for the correct aircraft.

We enter into the flight management computer the zero-fuel weight, which includes the airplane weight, the bags, the cargo, all the passengers, everything that we're going to fly with except for fuel.

Once the zero-fuel weight is entered, we enter the fuel weight in pounds. When the fuel weight is entered, we'll have a total takeoff weight for the aircraft. The takeoff weight of the aircraft can be compared to the takeoff performance section of the flight plan generated by the dispatcher.

There is a tape recording that we can either print or listen to on tape called ATIS, Airport Traffic Information Service, and this will give outside weather conditions, temperature, altimeter settings, closures of taxiways and ramp areas. The ATIS will also give departure and arrival runways in use. That will generally determine which departure runway we will use.

* * *

What Are the Pilots Doing During the Takeoff Roll?

This is another question I often get asked a lot. It is really our busiest time of flight. We know the aircraft meets performance requirements for the runway we are using, but we are very carefully monitoring power settings, making sure the engines are operating at the intended power setting, making sure the airplane is accelerating normally, as well as everything we would expect to see during the takeoff roll is happening when we expect to see it.

We also continuously watch to ensure our runway remains clear of traffic during our takeoff roll. While we're doing all of this, we're obviously also monitoring our speed to see when we arrive at V1.

V1 is takeoff decision speed. Prior to V1, the aircraft is able to stop on the remaining runway should the takeoff be rejected. After V1, the aircraft is able to continue the takeoff on one engine within the runway remaining and climb over close-in obstacles, such as buildings, along the extended runway center line.

If you ever have a chance to participate in our Cleared for Takeoff 301, The Flight Class, you will hear all of us cheer and throw our arms up in the air the moment we reach V1!

* * *

Who Determines How Much Fuel Is Going to Be Loaded Onto the Airplane for A Specific Flight?

This is another very popular question that is being asked by our students during every class. This is actually a complex process which the dispatcher performs along with flight and performance planning.

The first thing the dispatcher will consider is how much fuel it is going to take to get from point A to point B on the route that he has selected. He will start with that as a baseline fuel and will then start making additives.

One of the considerations he will start with first is calculating the amount of reserve fuel needed. This is the extra fuel we will have on our airplane. This will be dictated by many variables:

1. What is the weather forecast going to be?
2. Initially the dispatcher will include fuel for a minimum of 45 minutes' flying time.
3. If the weather conditions for the time of arrival are lower than prescribed minimums, the reserve fuel amount will include fuel to fly from the destination airport to an alternate airport, as well as usually an extra 30 -45 minutes of flying time past the alternate airport.

There are other standard levels of reserves added when the airplane is making a long flight.

4. The dispatcher then has a column where he can add fuel just because of variables that may arise on the route selection. We might have our route changed by air traffic control or might have an altitude change and there might be a history on that flight of these kinds of changes happening. He might add an extra amount if he thinks it's necessary for the flight.

There are other factors such as conditional aspects to the weather forecast or a single-runway airport.

Now the dispatcher has any additives he selected, alternate fuel, holding fuel, and en route fuel. Then on top of that, he will add taxi fuel which he will nominally base on the history of that flight. Once he adds the taxi fuel to all the above amounts, he then comes up with a total release fuel for the flight and the airplane will be fueled to that total amount.

This process that the dispatcher performs is called fuel buildup and at the end of it he knows precisely how much fuel is needed for a specific flight.

* * *

FLYING OVER WATER

Here at FearlessFlight® we periodically run free Flying over Water Webinars. If flying over water makes you a little nervous and you would like to know more about it, please take a moment and join our Flying over Water Webinar Notification list so that you will be informed when we are running this Webinar next:

* * *

Extended-Range Twin-Engine Operational Performance Standards (ETOPS)

ETOPS stands for Extended-range Twin-engine Operational Performance Standards, a rule which permits twin engine aircraft to fly routes which were formerly flown by 3 and 4-engine aircraft.

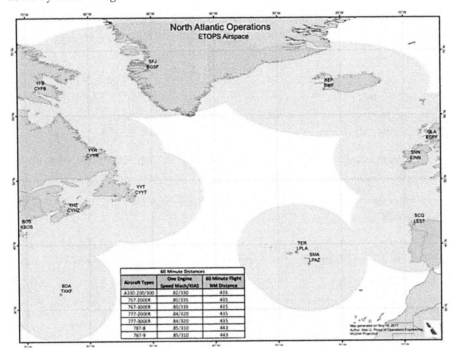

These routes may utilize alternate airports at distances up to 120, 180, or 207 minutes of flying time on a single engine from any point along the route.

ETOPS certification is a relatively recent addition to flying regulations. The airlines petitioned the FAA to allow them to operate aircraft over water with two engines instead of three or four and the petition and the basis of its approval was made on the reliability of the new generation of engines.

They were able to show via maintenance cycles and reliability tests that this was not compromising of safety. There is an extensive amount of planning made when we operate an aircraft overwater under ETOPS rules because of the reduced number of alternate airports that are landing alternates in the event of a diversion or emergency. Each flight has its own special dispatch desk. These dispatchers have special training that allows them to prepare flight plans for ETOPS flights.

Fuel considerations, alternate considerations, what, if anything, in the airplane that can be an inoperative is much more restrictive under an ETOPS release than a regular dispatch release.

We will address some flight considerations on the fixed Pacific tracks that extend from the West Coast of the U.S. to the Hawaiian Islands.

While we are on those tracks, we are not in radar contact with the air route traffic control center that manages our flight. In this case, that facility is the Oakland air route traffic control center. They have control of all the flights operating from the West Coast of the United States to Hawaii.

While we are established on these tracks and not in radar contact, we are making position reports at certain fixes that we cross every 45 minutes to an hour or so. Should our reported estimated time over the next fix differ, by plus or minus 3 minutes, we will update our ETA mid segment with Oakland.

In our example en route to Hawaii, we only have two options should we require an alternate airport. Prior to departure, the dispatcher has included in our flight plan an equal time point (ETP).

The ETP is the point in time on our track where returning to the West Coast of the U.S. or continuing to the Hawaiian Islands require an equivalent amount of time. Crossing that point West bound if a diversion is needed, we will continue to the Hawaiian Islands.

Prior to the ETP, if we need to divert, we will return to the West Coast of the U.S. We are able to make a diversion from this point on one or two engines.

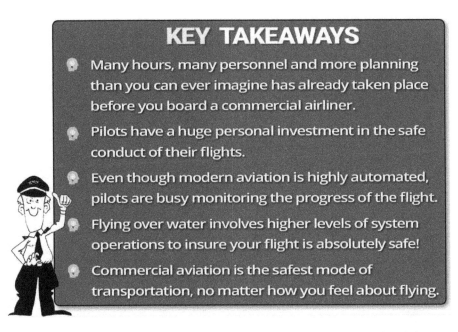

KEY TAKEAWAYS

- Many hours, many personnel and more planning than you can ever imagine has already taken place before you board a commercial airliner.

- Pilots have a huge personal investment in the safe conduct of their flights.

- Even though modern aviation is highly automated, pilots are busy monitoring the progress of the flight.

- Flying over water involves higher levels of system operations to insure your flight is absolutely safe!

- Commercial aviation is the safest mode of transportation, no matter how you feel about flying.

I hope that these past few chapters have helped you put your mind and fears at ease, now that you are armed with important and powerful knowledge about why exactly commercial aviation is the safest mode of transportation and that your fear of flying is a disorder because it is not grounded in reality.

Fear of flying has one of the highest rates of success when treated properly. Over the last 32+ years I helped many thousands of fearful flyers become fearless flyers.

I would love to have the opportunity to do the same for you.

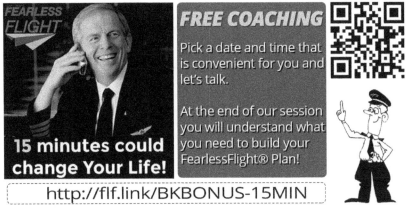

FEARLESS FLIGHT

15 minutes could change Your Life!

FREE COACHING

Pick a date and time that is convenient for you and let's talk.

At the end of our session you will understand what you need to build your FearlessFlight® Plan!

http://flf.link/BKBONUS-15MIN

PART 3

COPING TOOLS
AND STRATEGIES

Part 3 of the book is written to provide concrete tools and strategies that you can use to intervene in your current thinking to change the way that you think and manage your fear.

After you have completed Part 3, you will know how to:

- Understand exactly how to ACE your next flight
- Apply what you have learned to continue to grow and generate the confidence you need to fly fearlessly
- Open the door to living a truly limitless life and the freedom to travel whenever, wherever!

CHAPTER 11

HOW TO ACE YOUR NEXT FLIGHT

*"How can I choose differently when I
don't know what my choices are?"*

—CAPT RON

FEARLESS FLYING ACE

I think the most difficult challenge for man is becoming aware of that which he doesn't know that he doesn't know. We are born with the amazing ability to choose our own destiny. But this requires us to somehow raise our level of awareness. We are the only species that has a particular part of the brain mapped to observe our own thinking.

That's the good news and the bad news. The good news is when that thinking is positive, we experience joy and elation. The bad news is when that thinking is negative, we can suffer.

Why are we talking about this? It's because of the theme of this chapter is:

If you want to change your experience, you have to change your behavior. To overcome fear of flying, behavior change is the goal. This brings to mind the famous Einstein quote, *"Insanity is doing the same thing over and over and expecting a different result."* If you keep flying the way you have been (or avoiding flying altogether) without doing something different, you're going to continue to be miserable. As Dr. Phil likes to say, *"How's that working for you?"* So, what are you going to do to change?

Everybody and his or her brother is talking about mindfulness right now. Be careful. I want to give you a context for how I view mindfulness. It is in the context of increasing my awareness starting with that part of my brain that watches my thinking. It's sort of like being your own observer. Without an awareness that you are both the thinker and the observer, instead of just having a thought (which might generate a feeling), you risk *becoming* your thought.

This is where mindfulness comes in. You can become aware in this moment that you are having a thought and that it's just a thought that may or may not be true. We've already established that thoughts can be both positive and negative, but it's those negative ones that make flying miserable.

What's at the Bottom of All of This?

I had a recent coaching session with a fearful flyer. She had been immersing herself in the news, and not surprisingly, she had dredged up all this fear all the opinions about the Boeing Airplane Company's issues. Now, she's all freaked out because she wants to go to Spain, but she can't figure out which airplane to buy a ticket for.

She's also uncertain about which airline she should fly on because she doesn't know if the airline is safe. She doesn't know if the planes that the airline uses are safe. The stories in the media are full of experts—pilots, whistle blowers, employees, disgruntled employees, FAA inspectors, corporate CEOs. Who in the heck is she supposed to believe?

You'll recall that negative thoughts come from stories (Chapter 1), and stories come from thinking. So, we're back to the fact that you have to recognize that stories are just a collection of thoughts (what you believe), and you're just making it up as you go along! Remember, this is what the brain does. It is trying to protect you.

You have to figure out what to believe, and you also have to recognize your thoughts; you have to recognize them as just thoughts and not the gospel truth.

So, I said to this fearful flyer, *"Do you ever go to the grocery store in your car?"* Of course, she said she did. I asked, *"Have you ever heard that accidents are more likely to happen closer to home?"* She agreed that yes, accidents are likely to happen within a few miles of home.

Then I said, "*Do you check your tires before you get in your car to drive to the grocery store?*" She laughed and said no. "*Do you call up your city's traffic department and ask if all the traffic signals are working properly? Do you know if the other drivers on the street are properly licensed, in good health, and are sober? Do these drivers properly maintain their cars?*" She sheepishly said, "Well, no."

I asked her, "*Do you think that when you know all the answers to all the questions that you'll feel safe?*" I pointed out to her that she thinks she needs to know everything about flying before she flies in order to feel safe.

The reason that she's like this is because she's human. I suggested to her that these are yet more stories. She's even telling herself a story about driving: it's okay not to know anything ahead of time when she goes out in her car because she's done it every day for years and years, and nothing has ever happened.

And she thinks that if something happens, she's in control of her vehicle. Really?

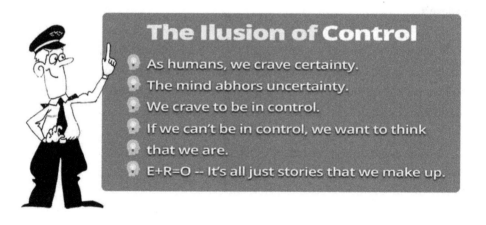

The Ilusion of Control

- As humans, we crave certainty.
- The mind abhors uncertainty.
- We crave to be in control.
- If we can't be in control, we want to think
- that we are.
- E+R=O -- It's all just stories that we make up.

Our discussion continued. I explained that the main difference between driving in your car and flying on an airplane is whole lot of government regulation control and compliance that the airlines cannot avoid.

I reminded her that she had already admitted that she didn't even check her tires before she drives! (Do you?) I pointed out that I always check the tires of my airplane before I take off and after I land, and I'm just an interested party of this complex system designed solely to keep you safe.

Even though I do my part, I'm not even in control of what goes on behind the scenes. Although I'm not in control, there is a system that I can trust to do things that I wouldn't even do for my own vehicle.

This brings up another issue:

Riding as a passenger on a major airline isn't about whether the airplane is safe. It's about our inability to trust.

We don't like it when we have to trust others, especially when we are relying on them to complete complex processes like building, maintaining, and operating airplanes. We're back to the problem of not being able to control our destiny. Welcome to the human race. Any thoughts that we can control those things outside our control are just illusions. Another illusion is that we can control anything or anyone. Bummer!

As I observed her reaction when I brought up trust, it occurred to me to ask her this: *"Has anybody ever disappointed you or broken your trust?"* Tears came to her eyes....

In reading just a few short paragraphs, you have very likely increased your awareness of some of the issues that bother you as a fearful flyer. My client wanted her fear to be about everything that she thought. She wanted the solution to be outside of her. She wanted it to be something you can take a pill for. These are the thoughts that she identified after our one hour coaching session.

Will this new awareness make her completely anxiety free in time for her next flight? Probably not. Will it make a difference? Probably.

Because of her new awareness, it is likely that she empowered "her observer" to recognize that those thoughts are just thoughts. And the feelings that might result from those thoughts are just feelings. And they will all pass. This particular fearful flyer now has some choices that previously she didn't even know existed. Now she has the opportunity to truly change her behavior, which will change her experience of flying on an airplane.

In Chapter 1 we learned that we have two separate systems interplaying for control of our behavior at any given moment. We often think we know things that we don't know—not because we are stupid, but because they are revealed by the nature of our mind and our thinking. I'm grateful for so much in my life, but one of the things I am most grateful for is my curiosity. Without curiosity, I would stagnate in my awareness.

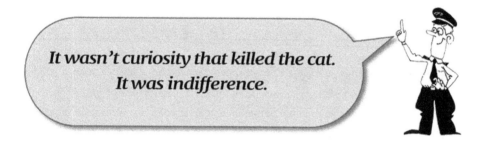

It wasn't curiosity that killed the cat.
It was indifference.

My curiosity drives my awareness, and in fact, I have realized that I have choices that I previously did not know existed. I did not know what I did not know. Once this was revealed, I could then truly make a choice. That has made all the difference in my life.

I've grown not only to love change, but also to seek it out. It's been an evolution. I wasn't born this way. It was something that I had to learn to appreciate. And I had to realize that change really isn't possible until I realized that I had other choices in my life. I became the master of my fate. Well, okay, busted. I'm still working on it.

If you want to master your fate, you have to learn how to become an ACE. To become an ACE is something of a tradition in aviation. An ACE is an expression from

WWI that signified a level of mastery in the skies. Originally it was a designation given to a fighter pilot for shooting down five enemy airplanes. I grew up thinking that courage was doing something heroic in combat. Having served in combat and watching fearful flyers overcome their fear has changed my mind. Heroism is a selfless act in spite of fear to defend oneself or others. But courage is moving forward in the face of fear. I am watching someone overcome their fear of flying inspires me in a way that combat did not.

* * *

To become an ACE and achieve mastery on your next flight you must nurture your curiosity:

- Start by educating yourself about fear and flying.
- Learn all you can.
- Make it fun.
- Replace myths about aviation with facts.
- Carry a small notebook and pen instead of an electronic device. Writing with your hand connects you to your brain in a way that is not necessarily the same as when using an electronic device.
- Note the sights, the sounds, and the sensations that you don't understand or that are unfamiliar.
- Record your feelings when they get triggered. Where in your body do you feel them? What do they feel like?
- Write with your non-dominant hand and notice how this slows down your thinking and calms your runaway mind.
- Take a breath while you're at it. Slow down your elephant. Let your rider do some work.

Remember:

Become your own observer during times of stress. Pay attention to where your attention is going. Learn to change your story.

Be mindful of your breath. Nothing is more direct in calming yourself than consciously slowing your rate of breathing. Learn to be more mindful. There's a lot of material available in books or even apps.

Learn how to let go of thoughts rather than clear your mind of them. For example, you're flying through turbulence. Inside of you, there's a little voice that's saying, *"I hate this. I can't do this. I can't stand one more minute of this! How much longer is it going to last?"* Crazy as it sounds, try taking the position of your observer and say to your thoughts, *"That's just a thought. That's just a feeling."*

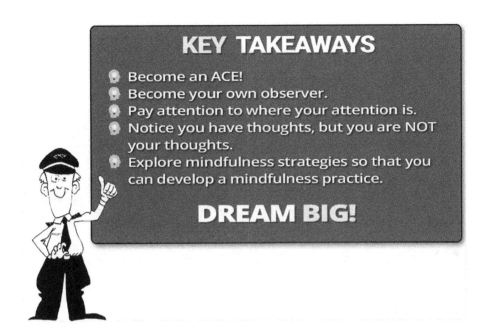

Dream…big! In the next chapter, you're going to imagine what it would be like to fly fearlessly.

Some of the best tips and tricks come from our very own **FearlessFlight® Birds of a Feather family**.

I created the group because I knew that social collaboration, being one of the three pillars of the **FearlessFlight® Method**, is really important in terms of connecting with other people, some of whom are still fearful flyers, others who have successfully overcome it and want to give back and support those still in the grip of their anxiety and fear.

My team and I contribute every day in some form in the group but what is truly inspiring is the care, comradery and consideration that members share with and for each other.

If you would like to find out more and join, simply scan the QR Code or type the link below into your browser on your smartphone, tablet or computer.

This is a caring, safe, supportive and inclusive group that welcomes all people trying to overcome their fear of flying and want to learn more about aviation and psychology!

Join Now

FearlessFlight
Birds of a Feather

MEMBERS ONLY

http://flf.link/BKBONUS-BOF

CHAPTER 12

WHAT WOULD IT BE LIKE IF YOU WERE NOT AFRAID TO FLY?

"Once you've overcome your fear of flying,
you're free to move about your life!"

—CAPT RON

I have experienced countless times that overcoming fear of flying brings joy and happiness to fearful flyers. Their newfound freedom leads to changes not only in the air but also on the ground.

Here Is an Example from One of My Clients:

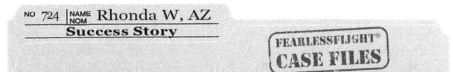

NO 724 | NAME/NOM Rhonda W, AZ
Success Story

FEARLESSFLIGHT®
CASE FILES

"It's 3:00 o'clock in the afternoon. I just finished making my airplane reservations. Now it begins. The anxiety, the sleepless nights, the constant thinking about getting on the airplane. Anxious thoughts that I can't seem to control or stop engulf my brain. It's all consuming.

"It's 3:00 o'clock in the afternoon. I just finished making my airplane reservations. Now it begins. The anxiety, the sleepless nights, the constant thinking about getting on the airplane. Anxious thoughts that I can't seem to control or stop engulf my brain. It's all consuming.

Flying was not an adventure for me. In fact, it was an experience that scared the crap out of me. I avoided it at all cost. Can I take a bus? Can I take a train? Heck, can I walk there?

I wasn't always this way. There was a time in my youth where I flew anytime, anywhere without a second thought. I flew to Okinawa twice, for goodness' sake! How did I become so afraid to get on an airplane?

Many of you may have always been afraid to fly. But if you are like me, there was a trigger that caused the onset of fearful flying. Mine was an extremely rough flight from Washington, D.C., to New York City. We flew in a thunderstorm, or at least I thought we were in middle of a thunderstorm. The plane bounced all over the place. Even the flight attendants looked scared. Not a good thing. That was in 1974. Everything changed from that one event.

As a result of this event and my fear of flying at age 24 (I'm now 68), I first flew with a few drinks under my belt before getting on the plane. That just made me feel horrible when I reached my destination basically because I was drunk. Then I took up Xanax. Not much help.

So, three years ago I took Capt Ron's 101 class at the Phoenix airport. With this class — along with his coaching, the FearlessFlight® Kit, watching his webinars and getting on many flights — I was able to successfully conquer my fear. It literally changed my life!"

I am always delighted when someone like Rhonda is able to overcome her fear of flying. I know how limiting and debilitating it can be. But for so many, the story of overcoming fear of flying doesn't end with what Rhonda refers to as being able "to conquer my fear." An act of courage such as Rhonda's can ripple outward to other aspects of life. Don't take my word for it. Rhonda's story continues happily onward and upward:

"The results of getting over my fear impacted every aspect of my life. I finally got the courage to divorce my husband of 47 years after years of trying. I lived alone for the first time in my life. I found the love of my life. I found joy and happiness, which I hadn't experienced in a very long time. So many things other than flying that I had been afraid to do, I did. These are just a few."

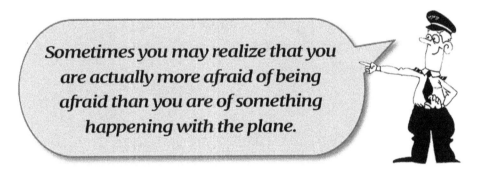

Sometimes you may realize that you are actually more afraid of being afraid than you are of something happening with the plane.

* * *

IMAGINE ALL THE THINGS YOU COULD DO IF YOU WEREN'T AFRAID TO FLY:

- You would look forward to booking a holiday abroad.
- You would stop dreading the journey home when you are halfway through your holiday.

- You would stop wasting your energy on negative thinking.
- You would no longer obsess about the noises on the airplane.
- You wouldn't have to worry planning a family vacation and would actually look forward to family travel.
- You would be free to accept a promotion that involves travel.
- You could apply for your dream job which involves flying.
- You could spend more time with the people you love and care about who live all over the country without having to worry about fear of flying there and back.
- You could take advantage of the opportunities to travel with friends and family instead of coming up with excuses.
- You could enjoy a lot more time for yourself at a destination instead of spending time driving there.

HOW DOES OVERCOMING FEAR OF FLYING RELATE TO YOUR LIFE?

- I would have the confidence to conquer other fears and anxieties that stop me from living my life more fully.
- It would allow me to say "YES" to my life.
- It would give me the courage to make and follow through with important life changes.
- The world opens up and becomes bigger.
- I am more capable of going outside my comfort zone and living life more fully.
- I would fulfill lifelong dreams.

SOME OF THE THINGS THAT PEOPLE DID AFTER THEY BECAME FEARLESS FLYERS:

- Visited Galápagos Islands
- Attended high school reunion
- Attended my mom's funeral
- Watched my son become a ballet impresario on the other side of the country
- Flew to my fiancée's homeland to accompany her back to the U.S. and married the love of my life (Actually, three different men have reported this to me!)
- Toured Europe
- Took advantage of a fellowship opportunity abroad
- Took advantage of a scholarship opportunity to study abroad
- Went on a company-sponsored reward trip to the Virgin Islands
- Took advantage of earning company incentives
- Attended weddings
- Cruised the Mediterranean
- Went on a dream vacation to Thailand
- Attended my own wedding in Austria

Use the Notes feature of your smart phone to list and record five things you'd like to do if you weren't afraid to fly.

* * *

KEY TAKEAWAYS

- Imagine all the things you could do if you weren't afraid to fly anymore!
- Get outta' your chair and into the air!
- An act of courage can ripple outward to other areas of your life!

ACTION PLAN:

Identify what the next right thing for you to do to overcome your fear of flying and then JUST DO IT!

STEP 1

If you haven't completed the research survey yet, please take a moment to head over to http://flf.link/IITOFOF_SURVEY and take inventory where you are at right now when it comes to your Fear of Flying. You can also scan the QR code below.

FEARLESSFLIGHT®
presents

Fear of Flying Research Study

Join thousands of fearful flyers and complete this Survey!

- Help find important answers about fear of flying
- Contribute to faster and more effective treatment options
- Increase awareness and service by airlines for fearful flyers

http://flf.link/BKBONUS-SURVEY

CHAPTER 13

THE TOOLS AND STRATEGIES FOR OVERCOMING YOUR FEAR OF FLYING

*"Fear of flying is the PERCEPTION of a life-threatening
event, situation, or circumstance combined
with feelings of helplessness."*

—CAPT RON

So, what's the Next Right Step for You to Take
To Overcome Your Fear of Flying?

You will find some of the most helpful tools and strategies in this chapter. A good strategy provides a clear roadmap and consists of a set of guiding principles which define the actions you should take (or not take) and the tools you should (or should not) use to achieve your desired goal. Your goal is to overcome your fear of flying, which you will ultimately accomplish by recognizing, regulating and replacing your negative mental dialogue with one that is empowering for you and generates the confidence you need when you get on an airplane next.

- A tool is a device, or in our case a concept, to use as a means to an end.
- A strategy is a plan of action designed to achieve a major goal and may use tools to implement this plan.

The FearlessFlight® Kit is a tool. Using it every night at bedtime is a strategy. Using it during the day when you find your anxiety climbing out of control is another strategy. Using it in the boarding area to silence the noise in your head is yet another strategy.

So, tools can be used with many different strategies. You may think of a strategy as your "game plan" but I prefer to call it your FearlessFlight® Plan.

I never fly anywhere without my Flight Plan, and neither should you.

Assessing Your Anxiety Level

Before we begin, take a moment and assess where your anxiety level is right now when it comes to flying.

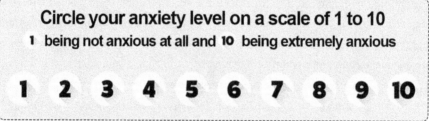

Circle your anxiety level on a scale of 1 to 10
1 being not anxious at all and **10** being extremely anxious

1   2   3   4   5   6   7   8   9   10

I have a saying that you are where you are. Whether you think of yourself as the worst fearful flyer or someone who's a hopeless case or someone who doesn't have it as bad as somebody else, you are exactly where you are today.

No judgments. Just accept the awareness of where you are.

My goal is to help you decrease your level of anxiety no matter where you are at this point, in order to make it more manageable for you to fly.

I do this by offering the following tools and strategies. My final goal is for you to build a FearlessFlight® Plan to use to help you manage your fear of flying.

I recommend that after you have put your FearlessFlight® Plan into action and taken your next flight that you reassess your anxiety level to see if it has come down from this original assessment.

I suggest that your first goal in overcoming fear of flying be to achieve improvement rather than an overnight miracle. This is where the assessment scale comes into play.

For example, after surgery when your doctor asks you to assess your pain on a scale of 1 to 10 and you say, *"It's a TEN!"* you'd be happy to get some relief from medication that brings your pain level down to a Five. As time goes on, you notice that your pain is lessening until one day when you notice that your pain is gone.

* * *

TOOLS

Just about any success story on FearlessFlight® makes mention of the **FearlessFlight® Harmonizer** and **FearlessFlight® Kit.**

The **FearlessFlight® Kit** is a collection of audio, video, and document files designed as tools to use in conjunction with strategies to overcome your fear of flying.

I designed it with the goal in mind to immediately and effectively relieve your stress related to anxiety, claustrophobia and other negative emotional sensations associated with fears of flying and flight phobia.

So, while the ultimate solution is to restore your mind's ability to focus your thoughts where YOU choose, the immediate goal is to break the obsessive-compulsive lock your mind has on your attention and move it to something less anxiety-producing. Think distraction.

Without being able to move your attention away from triggering thoughts and feelings, you will be forced to relive your anxiety over and over - sort of like in the movie Ground Hog Day.

The **FearlessFlight®** **HARMONIZER** is the only product available specifically for fearful flyers which uses bilateral brain stimulation and a form of hypnosis called "multi-evocation." It also has actual airplane sounds embedded to help desensitize your conscious mind while "drowning out" your anxiety-triggered self-talk that hijacks your brain. It starts the dialogue for you!

The FearlessFlight® Kit has been used successfully by thousands of people just like you!

The foundation of the **FearlessFlight®** **Kit** is the **FearlessFlight®** **Harmonizer** (FFH).

It was developed to "harmonize" those obsessive and usually compulsive thoughts that are automatically triggered by any events and circumstances associated with airplanes and flying.

Listen to Ronnie describe how his life changed, in large part because he used the tools and strategies, we teach here at FearlessFlight®, and specifically the Harmonizer.

Ronnie hadn't flown in 7 years (he's only 30-ish!). He believed that OTHER people could overcome THEIR fear, but felt he was a hopeless case.

* * *

NO 2098 | NAME NOM **Ronnie M, SC**
Success leaves clues!

FEARLESSFLIGHT®
CASE FILES

"Captain Ron,

Here I am starting my Monday and just last week I was doubting that I would ever see this day. Last week my brain started playing that familiar game with me where it was saying, "you aren't going to live to see next week.'

I think the biggest reward about yesterday is that I got to do the things that the little voice told me I wasn't going to be able to do. I got to watch Game 7 of the NBA Finals, Game of Thrones, and spend a nice evening with my wife and unimals.

Being in the air yesterday was amazing. I was particularly calm on the way back and got a feeling that I used to get. It was a feeling of how much I enjoy flying and how relaxing it really is.

I will never be able to truly express how much I appreciate what you have done for me...Your help gave me the confidence that I could do this and the reassurance that everything was going to be fine. Now every time I travel, I will always know that Captain Ron helped me get to wherever I traveled to. I am going to continue to listen to my flight harmonizer, exercise, listen to my motivational videos, and take your classes whenever I have the chance. I could type you a novel on how bad my fear WAS and how I told myself I would never fly again.

I will never forget the feeling I had yesterday when I got on the plane and I was contemplating getting off. I looked at the Southwest logo in front of me which had the wings with the heart in the middle. Out of nowhere I just felt this feeling of relief. I am going to need it to send you postcards for when Liz and I travel.

Thank you, thank you, thank you!

— RONNIE M.

Just as Ronnie found out, it is my sincere wish for you to recognize that success leaves clues and that with this book and the FearlessFlight® you will have what you need to regulate and replace your anxiety filled mental dialogue.

How to Use the Fearlessflight® Kit

- Use a headset and listen to audio and video volume as loud as you can stand it without causing hearing damage.
- Start listening to the **FearlessFlight®** **Harmonizer** 30 days before you have to fly, if possible.
- Load the **FearlessFlight®** **Kit** onto your device after purchase and listen to it once.
- Listen to the **FearlessFlight®** **Harmonizer** at bedtime, the first thing in the morning, and as necessary during the day.
- Listen to the **FearlessFlight®** **Harmonizer** whenever you have anxious thoughts about flying.

"Lean" into the Harmonizer as you immerse your conscious mind in a harmony of voices, music, and real-life sounds from a real flight.

Learn to Monitor and Control Your Breathing

Breathing is a requirement for life. For most of us, most of the time, it occurs without much thought. Each time we breathe in air, blood cells receive oxygen and release carbon dioxide. Carbon dioxide is a waste product that's carried back through your body and exhaled. Whenever our breath cycle is not functioning at its optimal level, the balance of the oxygen and carbon dioxide exchange is affected. This in turn can contribute to anxiety, panic attacks, fatigue, and other physical and emotional disturbances.

In general, there are two types of breathing patterns:

1. **Chest breathing (thoracic)**
2. **Abdominal breathing (diaphragmatic)**

When we are anxious, we tend to take rapid, shallow breaths that come directly from the chest. The resulting imbalance in the oxygen and carbon dioxide levels in the body leads to increased heart rate, dizziness, muscle tension, and other physical sensations. The lack of oxygen in the blood signals a stress response that contributes to anxiety and panic attacks.

DRINKING STRAW BREATHING EXERCISE

- Use a drinking straw to regulate your breathing
- Grab a handful (half a dozen or so) drinking straws when you go by one of the many food courts in the airport on the way to your gate
- Put the straw in your mouth and start focusing on your breathing — don't worry about how to breathe, put your initial focus on paying attention and slowing it down
- Now, look at your watch (or better yet, have a traveling partner / spouse / friend) and note the start time and count your breaths for a minute. Each inhale/exhale counts as one breath
- At the end of the minute, if you have more than 12-15 breaths per minute, start again. And if you have to, as you repeat and you notice that you're still breathing too fast, hold your breath briefly to artificially lower the count.
- When you get to 12-15 or lower, now continue to slow down your breathing and also begin to control the depth

- Continue to hold your breath at times if you notice your breathing rate speeding up

- Try to control your breath to the point that you slow it your rate to 6-9 breaths per minute—THE RATE AT WHICH IT WOULD BE IF YOU WERE HOME WATCHING TV OR READING A BOOK

- As you gain control, get out something to write with a journal your fears as they come up

- And, if you really want to take back control of your attention, put your pen in your non-dominant hand as you journal your fears. Your mind won't like it because it will be required to use more effort and concentration and can't have its way!

* * *

If you'd like to practice with a guided audio version of this exercise, simply scan the QR Code or type the link below into your browser on your smartphone, tablet or computer.

DRINKING STRAW BREATHING EXERCISE

FREE AUDIO

Listen to and enjoy this complimentary Guided Audio Version of the Drinking Straw Exercise.

A Guided Meditation is also included!

http://flf.link/BKBONUS-DSBE

STRATEGIES

CONTINUE TO EDUCATE YOURSELF ABOUT FLYING

Attend the *"Cleared for Takeoff"* Classes

If you are reading this and travel to the Phoenix or Los Angeles area is a possibility for you, I highly recommend you consider attending a class. You can find out more about the classes we offer on our website.

In my 32+ years of helping people overcome their fear of flying, the great majority of them actually are not local to either of these geographical areas. However, we are often livestreaming our free classes at Phoenix Sky Harbor airport, so that's one way for you to "attend" the class.

Watch Our *"How to Overcome Fear of Flying"* Online Masterclass

This class was professionally recorded and edited at the Air Hollywood, the world's largest aviation themed movie studio. My team and I condensed it into a 2-hour online video course consisting of 7 modules and 18 videos.

You can go through the material at your own pace, from the comfort of your own home or wherever you happen to watch it.

Watch and Listen to Our FearlessFlight® Weekly LIVE Show

It is the only weekly LIVE show dedicated to helping folks overcome their fear of flying. Every week, my wingman and First Officer here at FearlessFlight®, Dieter

Staudinger and I are discussing all things Fear of Flying. Most weeks my good friend and fellow pilot, Eric Larsen, who is still an active pilot for our nation's largest airline, answer your questions and discuss anything that may have happened during the week as it relates to aviation and flying. We frequently bring on guests as well to make it more interactive and provide more value to our viewers.

We are streaming **FearlessFlight®️ LIVE** to Facebook, YouTube and Twitter every Tuesday @ 6:30 p.m. Pacific. You can also watch previous episodes on our website.

Join the FearlessFlight®️ Birds of a Feather Facebook Group

We created the Facebook group because as you remember, Social Collaboration is one of the pillars of the **FearlessFlight®️ Method**. It is a caring, safe, supportive and inclusive group that welcomes all people trying to overcome their fear of flying and want to learn more about aviation and psychology!

My team and I are in there every day, but it is our members that are sharing their favorite tips, articles, videos and other recommendations that have helped them. People are asking for support and receive it and members are also sharing their successes and being celebrated by the group.

It is a great way to get started and I encourage you to apply to join our *Birds of a Feather* **Group.**

Watch Capt Ron's YouTube videos

We have a lot of videos on our YouTube Channel and also continue to curate playlists of videos in the area of aviation, mindfulness and more.

Subscribe to our YouTube Channel, so that you will be notified whenever we are uploading or adding a new video to our Channel.

Take Advantage of Online Coaching with Me

Private coaching is THE most effective treatment for fear of flying. It's personalized for you, to find the things that trigger YOUR fear, and get answers on how to control your anxiety, without drugs.

With over 32 years of experience and ongoing training in Professional Counselling, I have developed a knack to quickly develop strategies that work for you to finally get back onboard worry-free.

To see if coaching is a good option for you, schedule your FREE 15 minutes Coaching Consultation. Just pick a date and time that's convenient for you and let's talk.

Find a Support Partner

A support person can be your spouse, partner, friend, or anyone who can provide support for you before you fly and as you fly. Over three decades of fear of flying classes have left no doubt that those fearful flyers that have someone who supports them on their quest to overcome their fear of flying, generally do better. As you now know, social collaboration is one of the pillars of the FearlessFlight® Method.

We absolutely encourage it. Your friend, partner, husband or family member may not be afraid of flying but with our help they will learn exactly how to best support you.

They will also get a deeper understanding and appreciation of what you are going through and how they can learn to stop exasperating the situation and instead be a true support for you.

For those who don't have anyone around them that they would feel comfortable that could support them, we have created our FearlessFlight® Birds of a Feather Facebook group. Here you can connect with like-minded and like-hearted people who appreciate your struggles. Many of them have overcome their fear of flying and want to give back. Some of our members have even met up and flown together and lifelong friendships have developed. It is powerful and worthy of your consideration.

Flight Day Strategies

- Take your FearlessFlight® Harmonizer with you by making sure you all have all files loaded onto your device
- Arrive early at the airport (1½ to 2 hours prior to departure)
- Practice breathing in the boarding area
- Ask the gate agent to be able to pre-board

The Americans with Disabilities Act (and Air Carrier Access Act) provides for special boarding for passengers who need additional time boarding and special seating. Don't be afraid to ask!

- Advise Flight Attendants that you are a fearful flyer

- Ask to meet the pilots, *"Hi, my name is Ron. I'm a little nervous about flying. Could I meet the pilots?"*

- Speak to the pilots, *"Hi, my name is Ron. I'm a little nervous about flying. Any information you can tell me about the flight plan would be appreciated."*

- Be mindful. Focus only on the "present moment" not on the future and "what if" thinking.

- BE HERE NOW! In this present moment, you are safe, and you are okay. Remember that the present moment—and your response to it—is the only thing that you have control over.

- Remember to BREATHE!

ELITE CUSTOM COACHING PROGRAM

The best option for anyone who wants to get over their fear of flying in a minimum amount of time with maximum focus and an action plan that can fit it into their calendar and budget is my Elite Custom Coaching Program.

This program is by application only. As you can imagine, this option is popular for those who want to get on the fast track. Over the years, I have had the privilege to have flown with many great business leaders, actors, doctors and others from all across the country.

My team and I want to make sure that you are a good fit. We do this through the information that I glean from your application. I want to make sure you are ready for it and if you are, I will be able to provide you with a custom-tailored program that's designed for your maximum success. Guaranteed.

The highlight of the Elite Coaching Package is the Graduation Flight. We will schedule that during our first coaching session and ideally not more than 30 days from that date. And of course, the personalized attention and the first-class priority support you receive leading up to the flight will prepare you for nothing but success. This support is the pinnacle of all the one-to-one online/phone coaching that you and I will do prior to your flight. That, in turn, prepares you with the tools, strategies, and skills to nurture the confidence necessary to manage your anxiety and get you into the air.

I travel to meet you in person at an airport from which we can fly a roundtrip. The duration of our flight together will usually be within an hour to an hour-and-a-half away from your home airport. I will be coaching you while you practice and execute what you've learned during our individual coaching sessions leading up to the flight.

If you would like to find out more and apply for my Elite Custom Coaching Program, please simply scan the QR Code or type the link below into your browser on your smartphone, tablet or computer.

ELITE CUSTOM COACHING PROGRAM

BY APPLICATION ONLY!

The best option for anyone who wants to get over their fear of flying in a minimum amount of time with maximum focus and an action plan that can fit it into their calendar and budget is my Elite Custom Coaching Program.

http://flf.link/BKBONUS-ECCP

* * *

YOUR PERSONAL FLIGHT PLAN

It's always good to have a plan. If you do nothing before your next flight, don't expect anything to change.

> *"Those who fail to plan, plan to fail."*
> —H. K. WILLIAMS

We have created a sample **FearlessFlight® Flight Plan** for you. You can access this sample as well as **a FearlessFlight® Plan** Template to assist you in creating your own personalized plan for overcoming your fear of flying, simply scan the QR Code or type the link below into your browser on your smartphone, tablet or computer.

FearlessFlight® Plan Sample
http://flf.link/BKBONUS-FLIGHTPLAN

FearlessFlight® Plan Sample

FEARLESS FLIGHT

Date: August 16, 2019

Flight date: September 13, 2019

Flight Destination: Chicago

Triggers: Turbulence, airplane noises, takeoff

Trigger	Action Plan
Turbulence and takeoff	Download free copy of *Expert Turbulence & Takeoff Guide*
Feeling overwhelmed	Listen to the Flight Harmonizer before you fly and while flying
	Join the *Birds of a Feather Facebook* page to join a supportive community of like-minded flyers
	Message Capt Ron with questions
	When you board the airplane, ask to speak to the captain. Tell them you are an anxious flyer, and could they tell you something about the flight
Airplane noises	Message Capt Ron with questions about the noises you don't understand or make you feel anxious
	Book a free 15-minute coaching call with Capt Ron

v.1 8/16/19

"You're just ONE flight away!"

If you are still uncertain about exactly what your triggers are, remember that I have provided you with a Trigger Identification Exercise in Chapter 3. Use this exercise before you fill out your sample flight plan for maximum benefit of creating your own Personal Flight Plan.

KEY TAKEAWAYS

- If you so desire, my team and I here at FearlessFlight® are committed to serve and support you at any and every step on your journey to becoming fearless!!

GET YOURSELF CLEARED FOR TAKEOFF!

Implementing change requires you to make a choice. You don't have to make several choices today. In your quest to overcome your fear of flying, you just have to make one choice: to choose to do something differently today.

Be wary of anyone who says, *"Do this and your fear will vanish."* Fear of flying can be overwhelming. Overcoming your fear can seem impossible.

There's an old adage about how to eat an elephant: one bite at a time. Overcoming your fear of flying is a process. In this book, I've tried to help you find a place to make that first choice. Each fearful flyer's journey is unique. It's up to you to find your own path.

* * *

My 32 years of working with fearful flyers and witnessing the vulnerability that they have displayed has given me a tremendous compassion for the struggles people face in overcoming their fear.

I hope that the information you've read, the stories that I've shared, and the tools I've provided have moved you further along the path to FearlessFlight®.

I'm here to support you and provide any additional help that you need. I wish you all the best

and Happy Landings!

Capt Ron

GLOSSARY

Aviophobia: Fear of flying is a fear of being on an aeroplane (airplane), or other flying vehicle, such as a helicopter, while in flight. It is also referred to as flying anxiety, flying phobia, flight phobia, **aviophobia** or aerophobia (although the last also means a fear of drafts or of fresh air).

Mindfulness: The quality or state of being conscious or aware of something. A mental state achieved by focusing one's awareness on the present moment, while calmly acknowledging and accepting one's feelings, thoughts, and bodily sensations, used as a therapeutic technique.

Poly vagal theory: Specifies two functionally distinct branches of the vagus, or tenth cranial nerve. It serves to identify the relationship between visceral experiences and the vagus nerve's parasympathetic control of the heart, lungs, and digestive tract.

Vagal brake: The **vagal brake's** essential function is to regulate heart rate through the rapid inhibition and disinhibition of **vagal** tone to the heart. When the **brake** is applied, **vagal** tone increases and cardiac output is reduced promoting relaxation, self-soothing, growth and repair.

Neuroception: The term "Neuroception" describes how neural circuits distinguish whether situations or people are safe, dangerous, or life threatening. Neuroception explains why a baby coos at a caregiver but cries at a stranger, or why a toddler enjoys a parent's embrace but views a hug from a stranger as an assault.

YOU MADE IT!

Pat yourself on the back and say, "Congratulations" for having the courage to purchase and read this book.

If inside, however, are you saying to yourself, "I'm here, but I really don't think I can overcome my fear all by myself, all of us here at FearlessFlight® are delighted to serve and support you."

Simply scan the QR Code or type the link below into your browser on your smartphone, tablet or computer.

http://flf.link/BKBONUS-15MIN